OLYMPIAD WORKBOOK

AF362209

01 Learning Objectives

02 Multiple Choice Questions

03 HOTS (Achievers Section)

04 Model Test Paper

05 Answer Keys and Solutions

06 OMR Answer Sheet

Published by:

V&S PUBLISHERS

F-2/16, Ansari road, Daryaganj, New Delhi-110002
☎ 23240026, 23240027 • *Fax:* 011-23240028
✉ info@vspublishers.com • 🌐 www.vspublishers.com

Online Brandstore: amazon.in/vspublishers

Regional Office : Hyderabad
5-1-707/1, Brij Bhawan (Beside Central Bank of India Lane)
Bank Street, Koti, Hyderabad - 500 095
☎ 040-24737290
✉ vspublishershyd@gmail.com

Follow us on:   

BUY OUR BOOKS FROM: AMAZON   FLIPKART

© Copyright: *V&S* PUBLISHERS
ISBN 978-81-977325-1-5
New Edition

DISCLAIMER

While every attempt has been made to provide accurate and timely information in this book, neither the author nor the publisher assumes any responsibility for errors, unintended omissions or commissions detected therein. The author and publisher makes no representation or warranty with respect to the comprehensiveness or completeness of the contents provided.

All matters included have been simplified under professional guidance for general information only, without any warranty for applicability on an individual. Any mention of an organization or a website in the book, by way of citation or as a source of additional information, doesn't imply the endorsement of the content either by the author or the publisher. It is possible that websites cited may have changed or removed between the time of editing and publishing the book.

Results from using the expert opinion in this book will be totally dependent on individual circumstances and factors beyond the control of the author and the publisher.

It makes sense to elicit advice from well informed sources before implementing the ideas given in the book. The reader assumes full responsibility for the consequences arising out from reading this book.

For proper guidance, it is advisable to read the book under the watchful eyes of parents/guardian. The buyer of this book assumes all responsibility for the use of given materials and information.

The copyright of the entire content of this book rests with the author/publisher. Any infringement/transmission of the cover design, text or illustrations, in any form, by any means, by any entity will invite legal action and be responsible for consequences thereon.

PUBLISHER'S NOTE

V&S Publishers has carved a significant niche in the publishing industry over the last decade, having successfully published more than 1000 titles across 9 languages spanning over 50 subject categories. Being known for the quality of content, we have built a reputation of excellence and reliability. We have consistently delivered **"Value & Substance"** to our readers, through a wide range of titles across a variety of genres covering school books, fiction and non-fiction that caters to different people from every section of the society.

The **Olympiad Guidebooks for classes 1-10** across all subjects, launched almost a decade ago, under the **GEN X Imprint**, became a go-to-source for the school students in no time, owing to their invaluable and substantive content written in a guidebook pattern,.

Having successfully sold a million copies of the same and in response to demand by both students as well as shopkeepers nationwide; we now present before you our newly launched **Olympiad Workbook Series**, designed for **classes 1-10 across 4 subjects**.

The workbooks are meticulously curated by a team of experienced educators, researchers and subject matter experts, edited by professionals and peer reviewed by teachers. The team has poured its efforts and expertise into creating a crisp and concise workbook which will help and guide the students to the path of success in Olympiad exams. The **MCQs** identified will not only help in scoring top marks in Olympiads but also inculcate a sense of deeper understanding of the subject, by way of solving **HOTS** and referring to complete solutions at the end of the book.

Here we present our new release– **OLYMPIAD WORKBOOK (IMO) CLASS–8** having following features:

- ☞ Based on the latest syllabi
- ☞ MCQs with comprehensive coverage of topics
- ☞ HOTS Questions liberally included
- ☞ A dedicated chapter on logical reasoning
- ☞ Model test paper for thorough practice
- ☞ Sample OMR sheet for real time simulation

We have made sure through our best efforts, that this workbook strictly follows the latest syllabi and patterns of the Olympiad Examination.

As **V&S Publishers** continuously strive to enhance the readability and maintain the credibility of our academic publications, we seek the support of our valuable readers in influencing and enriching the lives of future generations of students.

P.S. While every care has been taken to ensure the correctness of the content, if you come across any error, howsoever minor, do not hesitate to discuss with teachers while pointing that out to us in no uncertain terms.

We wish you all the best for your exams!

DISTINCTIVE FEATURES

01

Learning Objectives

They list the whole chapter as subtopics, helping the teachers to guide children in a step-by-step manner.

02

Multiple Choice Questions

MCQs act as an excellent learning aid, helping you to understand and work on your mistakes.

03

HOTS (Achievers Section)

The High Order Thinking Questions aim to help the student to solve Application-based questions and gain practical understanding of the subject.

04

Model Test Paper

Model test paper are provided at the end of each book, which help the student to test the knowledge which they have gained after thorough reading of all chapters.

05

Answer Key

Detailed Answer Key along with explanations aid the pupil to indentify, understand the mistakes they make during the course of Olympiad preparation.

CONTENTS

RATIONAL NUMBERS

LEARNING OBJECTIVES

➤ Rational Numbers
➤ Terminating and Non-terminating decimals

➤ Properties of rational numbers
➤ Rational numbers between two rational numbers

MULTIPLE CHOICE QUESTIONS

1. The product of two numbers is $\dfrac{-16}{35}$. If one of the number is $\dfrac{-15}{14}$ what is the other number?

   (A) $\dfrac{16}{75}$

   (B) $\dfrac{32}{75}$

   (C) $\dfrac{64}{75}$

   (D) $\dfrac{8}{15}$

2. What should be subtracted from $\dfrac{-5}{3}$ to get $\dfrac{5}{6}$?

   (A) $\dfrac{-5}{2}$

   (B) $\dfrac{-3}{2}$

   (C) $\dfrac{3}{2}$

   (D) $\dfrac{-5}{4}$

3. What is additive inverse of $\dfrac{-7}{9}$?

   (A) $\dfrac{7}{9}$

   (B) $\dfrac{-9}{7}$

   (C) $\dfrac{9}{7}$

   (D) 1

4. The sum of two rational numbers is -3. If one of the number is $\dfrac{-10}{3}$. what is the other number?

   (A) $\dfrac{1}{3}$

   (B) $\dfrac{13}{3}$

   (C) $\dfrac{19}{3}$

   (D) $\dfrac{-19}{3}$

5. The cost of $7\dfrac{1}{2}$ metres of cloth is ₹ $78\dfrac{3}{4}$. What is the cost of one metre of cloth?

   (A) ₹ $13\dfrac{1}{2}$

   (B) ₹ $10\dfrac{1}{2}$

   (C) ₹ $16\dfrac{1}{2}$

   (D) ₹ $12\dfrac{1}{2}$

6. By what number should $\dfrac{-33}{8}$ be divided to get $\dfrac{-11}{2}$?

   (A) $\dfrac{1}{4}$

   (B) $\dfrac{1}{2}$

   (C) $\dfrac{3}{4}$

   (D) $\dfrac{1}{3}$

7. By what rational number should we multiply $\dfrac{-16}{63}$ to get $\dfrac{-4}{7}$.

(A) $\dfrac{7}{4}$ (B) $\dfrac{9}{4}$

(C) $\dfrac{3}{4}$ (D) $\dfrac{13}{4}$

8. What number should be added to $\dfrac{-7}{8}$ to get $\dfrac{4}{9}$?

(A) $\dfrac{75}{72}$ (B) $\dfrac{85}{72}$

(C) $\dfrac{83}{72}$ (D) $\dfrac{95}{72}$

9. What is reciprocal of $\left(\dfrac{1}{2}+\dfrac{1}{5}\right)$?

(A) $\dfrac{7}{10}$ (B) $\dfrac{10}{7}$

(C) $\dfrac{-7}{10}$ (D) $\dfrac{-10}{7}$

10. Which rational number is in between $\dfrac{-2}{3}$ and $\dfrac{-1}{4}$?

(A) $\dfrac{-5}{24}$ (B) $\dfrac{-5}{12}$

(C) $\dfrac{5}{12}$ (D) None of these

11. What is the reciprocal of $\left(\dfrac{1}{5}\times\dfrac{2}{5}\div\dfrac{4}{5}\right)$?

(A) $\dfrac{1}{10}$ (B) $\dfrac{1}{5}$

(C) 10   (D) 5

12. What should be added to $\dfrac{-3}{5}$ to get $\dfrac{-1}{3}$?

(A) $\dfrac{4}{5}$ (B) $\dfrac{2}{5}$

(C) $\dfrac{4}{15}$ (D) $\dfrac{8}{15}$

13. What is the additive inverse of $\left(\dfrac{3}{4}-\dfrac{2}{3}+\dfrac{1}{5}\right)$?

(A) $\dfrac{17}{60}$ (B) $\dfrac{-17}{60}$

(C) $\dfrac{60}{17}$ (D) $\dfrac{-60}{17}$

14. What is the value of $\dfrac{3}{4}\div\dfrac{5}{8}\times\dfrac{3}{7}+\dfrac{2}{9}-\dfrac{1}{3}$?

(A) $\dfrac{127}{315}$ (B) $\dfrac{117}{315}$

(C) $\dfrac{107}{315}$ (D) None of these

15. What is the value of

$$2-\left[5-\left\{4-\dfrac{3}{2}\left(2-\dfrac{2}{3}\right)\right\}\right]?$$

(A) 1   (B) –1

(C) 2   (D) –2

16. How many rational numbers lie between $\dfrac{1}{5}$ and $\dfrac{1}{3}$?

(A) One   (B) Two

(C) Three   (D) Infinite

17. If x is a non-zero rational number, then what is the value of x°?

(A) 1   (B) 0

(C) –1   (D) Not defined

18. Which number is the largest among the following numbers?

$$\dfrac{4}{-9},\dfrac{-5}{12},\dfrac{7}{-18},\dfrac{-2}{3}$$

(A) $\dfrac{7}{-18}$ (B) $\dfrac{4}{-9}$

(C) $\dfrac{-5}{12}$ (D) $\dfrac{-2}{3}$

19. Which number is the smallest among the following numbers?

$$\frac{-7}{12}, \frac{-5}{6}, \frac{13}{-18}, \frac{23}{-24}$$

(A) $\dfrac{-5}{6}$

(B) $\dfrac{-7}{12}$

(C) $\dfrac{-5}{6}$

(D) $\dfrac{23}{-24}$

20. Closure property of rational number will be valid for __________.

(A) Addition

(B) Subtraction

(C) Multiplication

(D) All of these.

21. Two octagonal perfect dice with numbers 1 to 8 are thrown together. What is the probability that both the numbers are even ?

(A) $\dfrac{1}{4}$

(B) $\dfrac{1}{32}$

(C) $\dfrac{7}{64}$

(D) $\dfrac{1}{2}$

22. One of the letters from the word SOCIOLOGY is chosen at random. What is the probability that this letter is O?

(A) $\dfrac{1}{3}$

(B) $\dfrac{1}{6}$

(C) $\dfrac{1}{9}$

(D) None of these

23. What is the simplified value of

$$\frac{1}{3} + \left[\frac{4}{9} + \left(\frac{-8}{13} \right) \right] \times \frac{169}{2} ?$$

(A) $\dfrac{-26}{9}$

(B) -2

(C) $\dfrac{-127}{9}$

(D) $\dfrac{-126}{3}$

24. How many rational numbers are there in between $\dfrac{3}{4}$ and 1?

(A) 0

(B) 1

(C) 2

(D) Countless

25. What should be subtracted from $-\dfrac{2}{3}$ to get -1?

(A) $\dfrac{1}{3}$

(B) $-\dfrac{1}{3}$

(C) $\dfrac{2}{3}$

(D) $-\dfrac{2}{3}$

1.	Ⓐ	Ⓑ	Ⓒ	Ⓓ	6.	Ⓐ	Ⓑ	Ⓒ	Ⓓ	11.	Ⓐ	Ⓑ	Ⓒ	Ⓓ	16	Ⓐ	Ⓑ	Ⓒ	Ⓓ	21.	Ⓐ	Ⓑ	Ⓒ	Ⓓ
2.	Ⓐ	Ⓑ	Ⓒ	Ⓓ	7.	Ⓐ	Ⓑ	Ⓒ	Ⓓ	12.	Ⓐ	Ⓑ	Ⓒ	Ⓓ	17.	Ⓐ	Ⓑ	Ⓒ	Ⓓ	22.	Ⓐ	Ⓑ	Ⓒ	Ⓓ
3.	Ⓐ	Ⓑ	Ⓒ	Ⓓ	8.	Ⓐ	Ⓑ	Ⓒ	Ⓓ	13.	Ⓐ	Ⓑ	Ⓒ	Ⓓ	18.	Ⓐ	Ⓑ	Ⓒ	Ⓓ	23.	Ⓐ	Ⓑ	Ⓒ	Ⓓ
4.	Ⓐ	Ⓑ	Ⓒ	Ⓓ	9.	Ⓐ	Ⓑ	Ⓒ	Ⓓ	14.	Ⓐ	Ⓑ	Ⓒ	Ⓓ	19.	Ⓐ	Ⓑ	Ⓒ	Ⓓ	24.	Ⓐ	Ⓑ	Ⓒ	Ⓓ
5.	Ⓐ	Ⓑ	Ⓒ	Ⓓ	10.	Ⓐ	Ⓑ	Ⓒ	Ⓓ	15.	Ⓐ	Ⓑ	Ⓒ	Ⓓ	20.	Ⓐ	Ⓑ	Ⓒ	Ⓓ	25.	Ⓐ	Ⓑ	Ⓒ	Ⓓ

LINEAR EQUATIONS IN ONE VARIABLE

2

LEARNING OBJECTIVES

➤ Concept of Linear equation in one variable

MULTIPLE CHOICE QUESTIONS

1. A boat goes downstream and covers the distance between two ports in 4 hours, while it covers the same distance upstream in 5 hours. If the speed of the stream is 2km/hour, what is the speed of boat in still water ?
   (A) 18 km/hour
   (B) 16 km/hour
   (C) 20 km/hour
   (D) 15 km/hour

2. The ages of Mohan and Sohan are in the ratio 9 : 7. Ten years ago their ages were in the ratio 7 : 5. What is the difference between their present ages?
   (A) 5 years   (B) 10 years
   (C) 15 years   (D) 20 years

3. The sum of two numbers is 360. If 65% of one number is equal to 85% of the other., which is the largest number among them?
   (A) 204   (B) 156
   (C) 256   (D) 214

4. A certain number of workers can finish a piece of work in 70 days. If there are 20 men less, it would take 10 days more for the same work to be finished. How many workers were there initially?
   (A) 150   (B) 160
   (C) 140   (D) 152

5. The sum of three consecutive multiples of 11 is 363. Which of these multiple is greatest?
   (A) 121   (B) 131
   (C) 132   (D) 122

6. Arun's age is three times his son's age. 10 years ago he was 5 times his son's age. What is the sum of their present ages?
   (A) 60 years   (B) 70 years
   (C) 80 years   (D) 90 years

7. Nirmal thinks of a number and subtracts 2½ from it. He multiplies the result by 8. The result now obtained is 3 times the same number he thought of. Find the number.
   (A) 4   (B) 5
   (C) 6   (D) 8

8. The difference between the digits of a two-digit number is 3. If the digits are interchanged and the resulting number is added to the original number we get 143. What was the original number?
   (A) 58   (B) 85 9
   (C) 78   (D) 87

9. A grand father is ten times older than his grandson. He is then also 54 years older than him. What is the sum of their present ages?
   (A) 66 yeas   (B) 45 years
   (C) 50 years   (D) 52 years

10. An altitude of a triangle is five-thirds the length of its corresponding base. If the altitude is increased by 4 cm and the base is decreased by 2 cm, the area of triangle remains the same. Find the base and altitude of the triangle respectively.

(A) 100 cm, 24 cm (B) 24 cm, 10 cm

(C) 20 cm, 12 cm (D) 12 cm, 20 cm

11. A field can be ploughed in 18 days. If everyday an additional area of 16 hectares is ploughed, the field can be ploughed in 12 days. What is the area of the field?

(A) 512 hectares (B) 576 hectares

(C) 528 hectares (D) None of these

12. The sum of the digits of a two digit number is 9. If 9 is subtracted from the number its digits are interchanged. What is the number?

(A) 54 (B) 63

(C) 72 (D) 45

13. What is the value of x in the given equatiom?

$$\frac{5(x+6)-15(2-x)}{3x-1}=10$$

(A) $x=1$

(B) $x=-1$

(C) $x=2$

(D) $x=-2$

14. What is the value of x in the given equation?

$$\frac{3x+1}{16}+\frac{2x-3}{7}=\frac{x+3}{8}+\frac{3x-1}{14}$$

(A) 2 (B) 3

(C) 4 (D) 5

15. What is the value of x if

$$\frac{x-n}{m+n}=\frac{x+n}{m-n}?$$

(A) m (B) n

(C) $-m$ (D) $-n$

16. A shirt is sold for ₹1498 and the seller gains 7% on it. What is the cost price of the shirt ?

(A) 1600 (B) 1500

(C) 1400 (D) 1450

17. Half of a herd of deer are grazing in the field and three fourth of remaining are playing nearby. The rest nine are drinking water from the river. What is the number of deer in the herd?

(A) 72 (B) 62

(C) 74 (D) 80

18. The ages of Raju and Rajan are in the ratio 5 : 8. If Raju was 5 years older and Rajan 4 years younger, the age of Raju would have been the same as that of Rajan. What is the age of Raju?

(A) 15 years (B) 16 years

(C) 24 years (D) 13 years

19. If $\frac{1}{2}$ is subtracted from a number and the difference is multiplied by 8, the result is 12. What is the number?

(A) 2 (B) 3

(C) 4 (D) 8

20. Mahesh travelled $\frac{1}{8}$th of his journey by bus, $\frac{1}{4}$th by taxi, $\frac{3}{5}$th by train and remaining 8 km by foot. What is the distance of his total journey?

(A) 120 km (B) 240 km

(C) 220 km (D) 320 km

21. The age of the father is three times the age of the son. If the age of the son is 15 years old, then the age of the father is:

    (A) 50 years (B) 55 years
    (C) 40 years (D) 45 years

22. The difference between two whole numbers is 66. The ratio of the two numbers is 2 : 5. The two numbers are:

    (A) 60 and 6 (B) 100 and 33
    (C) 110 and 44 (D) 99 and 33

23. If a number is divided by 8 it gives 6 as the value. Find the number.

    (A) 36 (B) 42
    (C) 48 (D) 56

24. When 75% of a number is added to 75 the result is the number again. What is the number?

    (A) 150 (B) 300
    (C) 100 (D) 450

25. A student has to secure 40% marks to pass. He got 30 marks and failed by 50 marks. What is the maximum number of marks?

    (A) 160
    (B) 180
    (C) 200
    (D) 320

Darken Your Choice with HB Pencil

1.	Ⓐ Ⓑ Ⓒ Ⓓ	6.	Ⓐ Ⓑ Ⓒ Ⓓ	11.	Ⓐ Ⓑ Ⓒ Ⓓ	16.	Ⓐ Ⓑ Ⓒ Ⓓ	21.	Ⓐ Ⓑ Ⓒ Ⓓ
2.	Ⓐ Ⓑ Ⓒ Ⓓ	7.	Ⓐ Ⓑ Ⓒ Ⓓ	12.	Ⓐ Ⓑ Ⓒ Ⓓ	17.	Ⓐ Ⓑ Ⓒ Ⓓ	22.	Ⓐ Ⓑ Ⓒ Ⓓ
3.	Ⓐ Ⓑ Ⓒ Ⓓ	8.	Ⓐ Ⓑ Ⓒ Ⓓ	13.	Ⓐ Ⓑ Ⓒ Ⓓ	18.	Ⓐ Ⓑ Ⓒ Ⓓ	23.	Ⓐ Ⓑ Ⓒ Ⓓ
4.	Ⓐ Ⓑ Ⓒ Ⓓ	9.	Ⓐ Ⓑ Ⓒ Ⓓ	14.	Ⓐ Ⓑ Ⓒ Ⓓ	19.	Ⓐ Ⓑ Ⓒ Ⓓ	24.	Ⓐ Ⓑ Ⓒ Ⓓ
5.	Ⓐ Ⓑ Ⓒ Ⓓ	10.	Ⓐ Ⓑ Ⓒ Ⓓ	15.	Ⓐ Ⓑ Ⓒ Ⓓ	20.	Ⓐ Ⓑ Ⓒ Ⓓ	25.	Ⓐ Ⓑ Ⓒ Ⓓ

QUADRILATERALS

LEARNING OBJECTIVES

➤ Basics of quadrilateral and its related concept
➤ Trapezium

MULTIPLE CHOICE QUESTIONS

1. The bisectors of any two adjacent angles of a parallelogram intersect at
   (A) 30°
   (B) 45°
   (C) 60°
   (D) 90°

2. If one angle of a parallelogram is 24° less than twice the smallest angle then what is the value of largest angle of the parallelogram?
   (A) 102°
   (B) 112°
   (C) 116°
   (D) 120°

3. The ratio of two sides of a parallelogram is 4 : 3. If its perimeter is 56 cm, what is the difference between largest and smallest side?
   (A) 8 cm
   (B) 4 cm
   (C) 12 cm
   (D) 16 cm

4. In the given Fig. ABCD is a rhombus. If ∠DMC = 90⁰, ∠DAB = 110°, what is ∠BDC ?

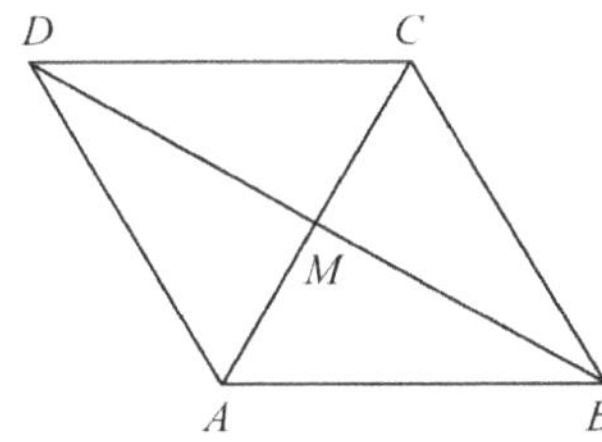

   (A) 30°
   (B) 35°
   (C) 40°
   (D) 45°

5. Two adjacent sides of a parallelogram are 5 cm and 7 cm long what is the perimeter of parallelogram?
   (A) 24 cm
   (B) 28 cm
   (C) 22 cm
   (D) 26 cm

6. Of any two adjacent sides of a parallelogram one is longer than the other by 3 cm. If the perimeter is 36 cm, then what is the length of smaller side of parallelogram?
   (A) 10.5 cm
   (B) 7.5 cm
   (C) 6 cm
   (D) 12 cm

7. ABCD is a rhombus, AC = 24 cm and BD = 10 cm, then what is the measure of BC?

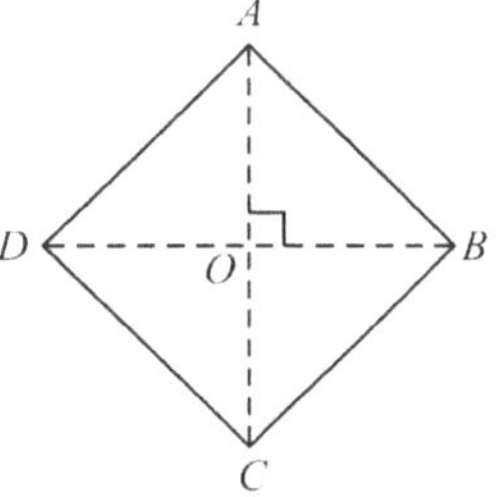

   (A) 13 cm
   (B) 12cm
   (C) 9 cm
   (D) 11 cm

8. In ΔBCE, BE = EC, and ABCD is a square, and ∠BEC = 60°, then the measure of ∠BEA will be :

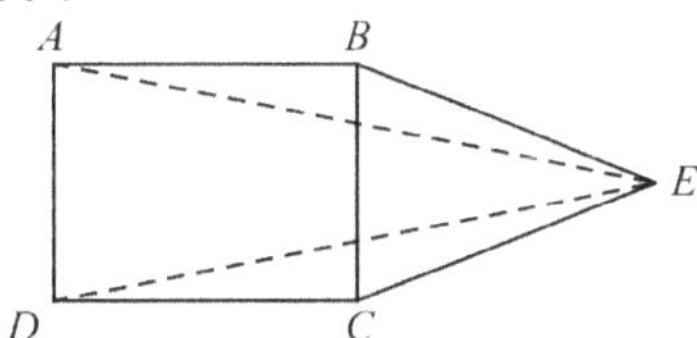

(A) 45° (B) 35°
(C) 15° (D) 25°

9. From the adjoining figure, find the measure of $\angle EFD$ if $AB \parallel CD$, $EF \parallel BC$.

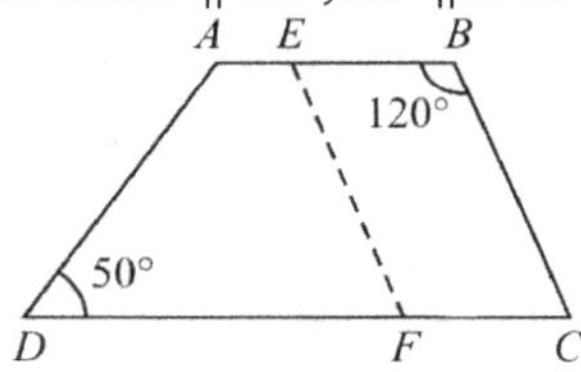

(A) 40° (B) 70°
(C) 50° (D) 60°

10. In the adjoining figure $ABCD$, $AD = DC$ and $AB = BC$ and, $\angle ADC = 40°$ and $\angle BCD = 140°$, then, $\angle ABC =$

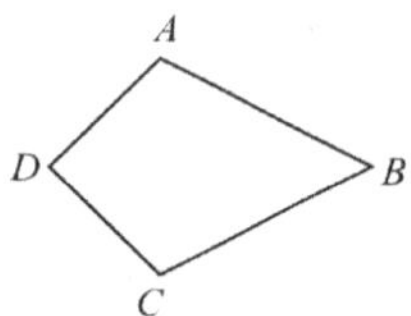

(A) 60° (B) 70°
(C) 40° (D) 50°

11. $ABCD$ is a parallelogram having its sides, $AB = 3x + 1$ $BC = 2y + 3$, $CD = 25$, $DA = y + 28$, then, $x + y =$

(A) 29 (B) 21
(C) 25 (D) 33

12. $PQRS$ is a parallelogram and $\angle SPR = 50°$, then find y.

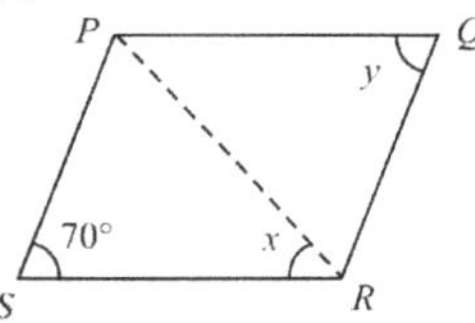

(A) 70° (B) 110°
(C) 50° (D) 130°

13. If $\alpha < 90°$, then, $ABCD$, may be a : (Given : $ABCD$ is a parallelogram and $\angle B = 90°$)

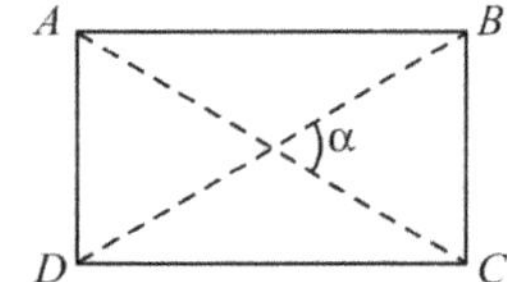

(A) Rectangle (B) Trapezium
(C) Square (D) Rhombus

14. If $\theta = 90°$, and, $\angle A = \angle C = 110°$, then, $ABCD$ is :

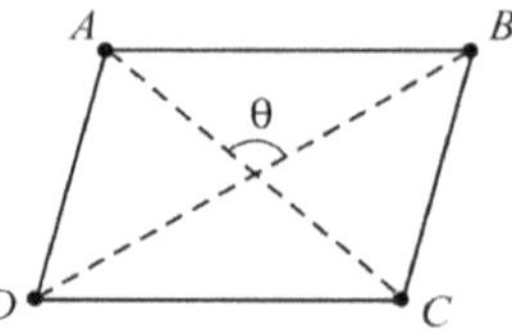

(A) Square (B) Rectangle
(C) Rhombus (D) None of these

15. $ABCD$ is an isosceles trapezium , i.e., $AD = BC$, then

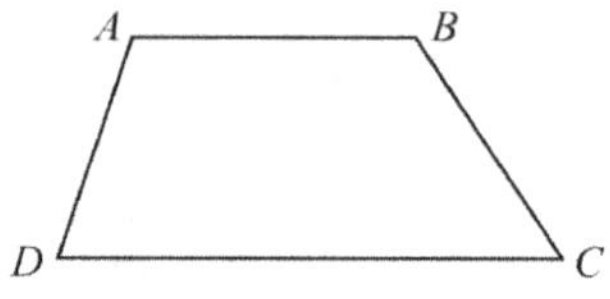

(A) $AD = CD$ (B) $\angle A = \angle B$
(C) $\angle A = \angle D$ (D) $\angle C = \angle A$

16. In the given figure, $OS = OQ$ and $PR = 2OP = 2OR$, and also, $OR = OS$, then, $PQRS$ is not a

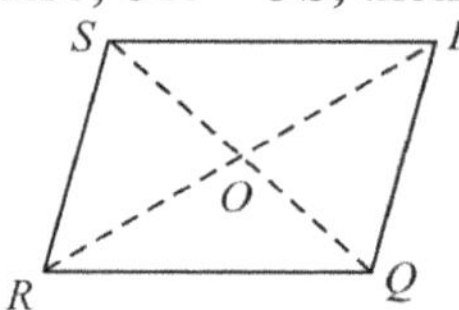

(A) Rhombus (B) Rectangle
(C) Square (D) Parallelogram.

17. In the adjoining figure, $AD \parallel BC$ and AB and DC are not parallel, then $\angle B =$

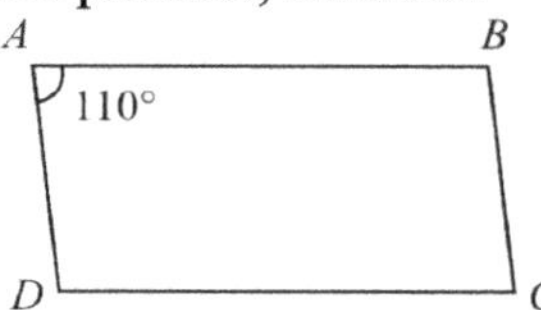

(A) 110° (B) 70°
(C) 80° (D) 40°

18. Find x and y:

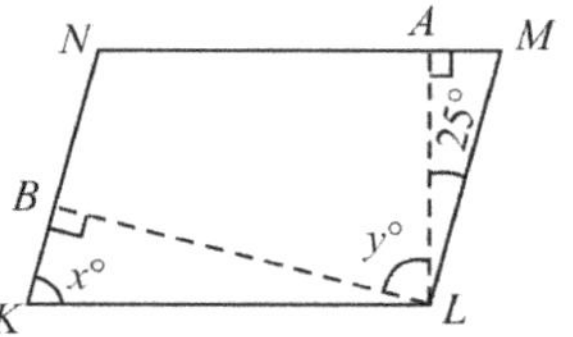

$KLMN$ is a parallelogram.
(A) $x = 55°, y = 55°$ (B) $x = 65°, y = 55°$
(C) $x = 60°, y = 65°$ (D) None of these

19. *ABCD* is a parallelogram.

The measure of $\angle ADO$ is :

(A) 55° (B) 45°

(C) 35° (D) 75°

20. The quadrilateral formed by joining the mid-points of a given quadrilateral will be (surely) :

(A) Parallelogram (B) Rectangle

(C) Rhombus (D) Square

HOTS (ACHIEVERS SECTION)

21. In a parallelogram ABCD, angle A and angle B are in the ratio 1:2. Find the angle A.

(A) 30° (B) 45°

(C) 60° (D) 90°

22. The angles of a quadrilateral are in ratio 1:2:3:4. Which angle has the largest measure?

(A) 120° (B) 144°

(C) 98° (D) 36°

23. The diagonals of a rectangle are $2x + 1$ and $3x - 1$, respectively. Find the value of x.

(A) 1 (B) 2

(C) 3 (D) 4

24. ABCD is a parallelogram. If angle A is equal to 45°, then find the measure of its adjacent angle.

(A) 135° (B) 120°

(C) 115° (D) 180°

25. If angles P, Q, R and S of the quadrilateral PQRS, taken in order, are in the ratio 3:7:6:4, what is PQRS?

(A) A rhombus (B) A parallelogram

(C) A trapezium (D) A kite

—Darken Your Choice with HB Pencil—

1.	Ⓐ Ⓑ Ⓒ Ⓓ	6.	Ⓐ Ⓑ Ⓒ Ⓓ	11.	Ⓐ Ⓑ Ⓒ Ⓓ	16	Ⓐ Ⓑ Ⓒ Ⓓ	21.	Ⓐ Ⓑ Ⓒ Ⓓ
2.	Ⓐ Ⓑ Ⓒ Ⓓ	7.	Ⓐ Ⓑ Ⓒ Ⓓ	12.	Ⓐ Ⓑ Ⓒ Ⓓ	17.	Ⓐ Ⓑ Ⓒ Ⓓ	22.	Ⓐ Ⓑ Ⓒ Ⓓ
3.	Ⓐ Ⓑ Ⓒ Ⓓ	8.	Ⓐ Ⓑ Ⓒ Ⓓ	13.	Ⓐ Ⓑ Ⓒ Ⓓ	18.	Ⓐ Ⓑ Ⓒ Ⓓ	23.	Ⓐ Ⓑ Ⓒ Ⓓ
4.	Ⓐ Ⓑ Ⓒ Ⓓ	9.	Ⓐ Ⓑ Ⓒ Ⓓ	14.	Ⓐ Ⓑ Ⓒ Ⓓ	19.	Ⓐ Ⓑ Ⓒ Ⓓ	24.	Ⓐ Ⓑ Ⓒ Ⓓ
5.	Ⓐ Ⓑ Ⓒ Ⓓ	10.	Ⓐ Ⓑ Ⓒ Ⓓ	15.	Ⓐ Ⓑ Ⓒ Ⓓ	20.	Ⓐ Ⓑ Ⓒ Ⓓ	25.	Ⓐ Ⓑ Ⓒ Ⓓ

PRACTICAL GEOMETRY

LEARNING OBJECTIVES

➤ Construction of quadrilaterals
➤ Line segment

MULTIPLE CHOICE QUESTIONS

1. The quadrilateral whose opposite sides are parallel is a ___________.
   (A) Parallelogram   (B) Triangle
   (C) None of these   (D) Quadrilateral

2. Polygons that have no portions of their diagonals in their exteriors are called ___________.
   (A) concave   (B) convex
   (C) squares   (D) triangles

3. A polygon with minimum number of sides is ___________.
   (A) triangle   (B) angle
   (C) square   (D) pentagon

4. All the sides of a regular polygon are ___________.
   (A) not equal   (B) equal
   (C) not parallel   (D) parallel

5. A simple closed curve made up of only ___________ is called a polygon .
   (A) line segments   (B) curves
   (C) lines   (D) closed curves

6. The park in a town is made in the form of a kite. Its perimeter is 90 metres and one side is 10 m more than other side. What are the lengths of all sides?
   (A) 20 m, 20 m, 29 m and 29 m
   (B) 20 m, 20 m, 27.5 m and 27.5 m
   (C) 17.5 m, 17.5 m, 29 m and 29 m
   (D) 17.5 m, 17.5 m, 27.5 m and 27.5 m

7. The ratio of two adjacent sides of a parallelogram is 4:5. If its perimeter is 72 cm, find its adjacent sides.
   (A) 18 cm and 25 cm
   (B) 18 cm and 20 cm
   (C) 16 cm and 20 cm
   (D) 16 cm and 25 cm

8. The quadrilateral whose diagonals are equal and bisect each other at right angle is ___________.
   (A) Triangle   (B) Rhombus
   (C) Square   (D) None of these

9. All the angles of a regular polygon are of ___________.
   (A) equal measure   (B) 90°
   (C) 60°   (D) equal length

10. Maximum number of right angles in a right angled triangle are___________.
    (A) 0   (B) 3
    (C) 2   (D) 1

11. Given below are the steps of construction to construct a quadrilateral ABCD where AB = 5.6 cm, BC = 4.1 cm, CD = 4.4 cm, AD = 3.3 cm and $\angle A$=75°.

    Which of the following steps is INCORRECT?

    Step 1: Draw AB = 5.6 cm and construct $\angle$BAX=75°.

    Step 2: With A as centre and radius = 3.3 cm, cut off AD = 3.3 cm along AX.

Step 3: Join BD. With D as centre and radius = 4.1 cm, draw an arc.

Step 4: With B as centre and radius = 4.1cm, draw an arc to cut the arc drawn in above step at C. Join BC, CD to obtain the required quadrilateral ABCD.

(A) Step 1 only   (B) Step 2 only

(C) Step 3 only   (D) Step 4 only

12. It is possible to construct a quadrilateral with the sufficient data (other than five simple cases), where less than ____ parts but some other relations between them are given.

(A) Four   (B) Five

(C) Three   (D) Two

13. Arrange the steps of construction while constructing a parallelogram ABCD, given that AB = 5 cm, BC = 4 cm and $\angle$B = 60°.

   1. With A as centre and radius equal to 4 cm, draw an arc cutting AY at D.

   2. At A, draw $\angle$YAB = 120°. [$\because$ A + B = 180°]

   3. At B, draw $\angle$XBA = 60°.

   4. Draw AB = 5cm.

   5. Join C(D)

   6. With B as centre and radius equal to 4 cm, drawn an arc cutting BX at C.

(A) 4, 3, 6, 2, 1, 5   (B) 4, 3, 2, 6, 5, 1

(C) 4, 6, 3, 1, 2, 5   (D) 4, 3, 6, 2, 5, 1

14. Arrange the steps of construction while constructing a quadrilateral ABCD given AB = 5.1 cm, AO = 4 cm, BC = 2.5 cm, $\angle$A = 60° and $\angle$B = 85°.

Step 1: With B as centre and radius 2.5 cm, cut off BC = 2.5 cm along BY.

Step 2 : Construct $\angle$XAB = 60° at A.

Step 3: Join CD.

Step 4: With A as centre and radius 4cm, cut off AD = 4 cm along AX.

Step 5: Draw AB = 5.1 cm.

Step 6: Construct $\angle$ABY = 85° at B.

(A) 5, 2, 4, 1, 3, 6   (B) 5, 4, 2, 1. 6, 3

(C) 5, 2, 4, 6, 1, 3   (D) 5, 2, 4, 1, 6, 3

15. If AB||DC, AB = 7cm, BC = 6cm, AD = 6.5 cm and $\angle$B = 70°, then which figure can be constructed?

(A) Square   (B) Trapezium

(C) Rhombus   (D) Rectangle

16. Given below are the steps of construction of a quadrilateral ABCD, where AB = 3.5 cm, BC = 6.5 cm, $\angle$A = 75°, $\angle$B = 105° and $\angle$C = 120°. Which of the following steps is INCORRECT?

Step 1: Draw AB = 3.5cm.

Step 2: Draw $\angle$XAB = 75° at A and $\angle$ABY = 105° at B.

Step 3: With B as centre and radius BC = 6.5 cm, draw an arc to intersect BV at C.

Stap 4: At C, draw $\angle$ADC = 120° such that CZ meets AX at D.

(A) Step 1 only   (B) Step 2 only

(C) Step 3 only   (D) Step 4 only

17. Which of the following statements is true about the construction of a quadrilateral where AB = 3 cm, BC = 5 cm, AC = 9 cm, AD = 6 cm. CD = 2 cm?

(A) It is possible to draw the quadrilateral.

(B) It is not possible to draw the quadrilateral, since AD ÷ DC < AC.

(C) It is possible to draw the quadrilateral, since AD + DC < AC

(D) None of these

18. To construct a quadrilateral ABCD, which of the following parts is necessary?

(A) Length of AB

(B) Length of BC

(C) Measure of $\angle$A, $\angle$B and $\angle$C

(D) All of these

19. Which of the given properties of a parallelogram is necessary to construct it?

(A) Opposite sides of a parallelogram

(B) Opposite angles of a parallelogram

(C) Diagonals of a parallelogram

(D) Both (A) and (B)

20. To construct a quadrilateral uniquely, it is necessary to have the knowledge of a least ____________ independent elements.

(A) Four   (B) Five

(C) Three   (D) Six

21. Which of the following statement is/are correct?

    We can construct a quadrilateral:
    (A) when its opposite sides are given
    (B) when its four angles and a side are given
    (C) when its diagonals are given
    (D) when its three angles and any two adjacent sides are given

22. Is it possible to construct a rhombus with its diagonals equal to its side?
    (A) No   (B) Sometimes
    (C) Always   (D) Can't say

23. We can construct a rhombus if its _________ are given.
    (A) side   (B) diagonals
    (C) angle   (D) None of these

24. Which type of quadrilateral is this.

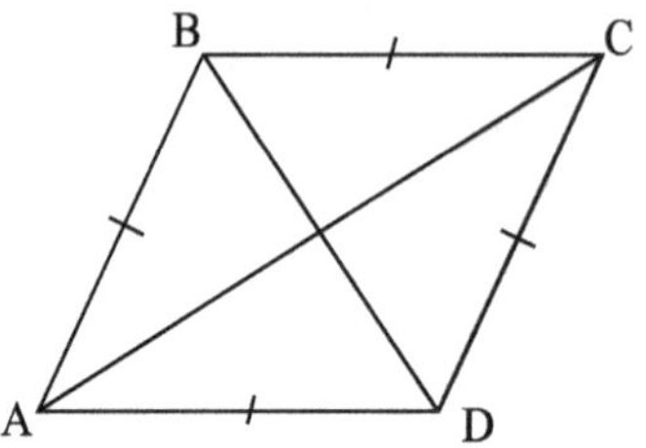

    (A) Rhombus   (B) Rectangle
    (C) Trapezium   (D) Kite

25. Construct a rectangle ABCD, when its sides are 6cm and 7.2 cm.

    Then, relation between diagonals AC and BD is:
    (A) AC = BD   (B) AC<BD
    (C) AC>BD   (D) Cannot say

1.	Ⓐ Ⓑ Ⓒ Ⓓ	6.	Ⓐ Ⓑ Ⓒ Ⓓ	11.	Ⓐ Ⓑ Ⓒ Ⓓ	16	Ⓐ Ⓑ Ⓒ Ⓓ	21.	Ⓐ Ⓑ Ⓒ Ⓓ
2.	Ⓐ Ⓑ Ⓒ Ⓓ	7.	Ⓐ Ⓑ Ⓒ Ⓓ	12.	Ⓐ Ⓑ Ⓒ Ⓓ	17.	Ⓐ Ⓑ Ⓒ Ⓓ	22.	Ⓐ Ⓑ Ⓒ Ⓓ
3.	Ⓐ Ⓑ Ⓒ Ⓓ	8.	Ⓐ Ⓑ Ⓒ Ⓓ	13.	Ⓐ Ⓑ Ⓒ Ⓓ	18.	Ⓐ Ⓑ Ⓒ Ⓓ	23.	Ⓐ Ⓑ Ⓒ Ⓓ
4.	Ⓐ Ⓑ Ⓒ Ⓓ	9.	Ⓐ Ⓑ Ⓒ Ⓓ	14.	Ⓐ Ⓑ Ⓒ Ⓓ	19.	Ⓐ Ⓑ Ⓒ Ⓓ	24.	Ⓐ Ⓑ Ⓒ Ⓓ
5.	Ⓐ Ⓑ Ⓒ Ⓓ	10.	Ⓐ Ⓑ Ⓒ Ⓓ	15.	Ⓐ Ⓑ Ⓒ Ⓓ	20.	Ⓐ Ⓑ Ⓒ Ⓓ	25.	Ⓐ Ⓑ Ⓒ Ⓓ

DATA HANDLING

LEARNING OBJECTIVES

➤ Types of Data
➤ Random Probability Concepts

MULTIPLE CHOICE QUESTIONS

1. From a well shuffled deck of 52 cards, one card is drawn at random. What is the probability that the card drawn is a diamond?

   (A) $\dfrac{1}{2}$ (B) $\dfrac{1}{3}$

   (C) $\dfrac{1}{4}$ (D) $\dfrac{1}{13}$

2. A bag contains 4 red balls, 5 green balls and 7 black balls. They are mixed thoroughly and one ball is drawn at random. What is the probability of getting a black ball?

   (A) $\dfrac{7}{16}$ (B) $\dfrac{5}{16}$

   (C) $\dfrac{1}{4}$ (D) $\dfrac{1}{16}$

3. The following data shows the agricultural production in India during a certain year.

Foodgrains	Rice	Wheat	Pulses	Maize
Production in million of tons	57	76	19	38

   What is the central angle for Rice in a pie chart?

   (A) 120°   (B) 108°
   (C) 90°   (D) 144°

4. The electricity bill in Rupees of 24 houses of a certain locality for a month are given below.
   472, 763, 312, 630, 584, 324, 700, 617, 754, 776, 596, 745, 565, 780, 378, 570, 685, 400, 356, 365, 435, 506, 548, 736.

   Arrange the data in increasing order and find the frequency of the group 700-800.

   (A) 3   (B) 4
   (C) 5   (D) 7

5. The monthly income of a family is ₹ 14, 400 and the central angle for the rent on a pie chart is 100°. What amount shows the rent?

   (A) ₹ 5400   (B) ₹ 1800
   (C) ₹ 4000   (D) ₹ 3600

6. In a pie-chart for expenditure in percent incurred in the construction of a house in a city, the central angle for cement is 72°. What is the percentage of cement expenditures ?

   (A) 15%   (B) 20%
   (C) 25%   (D) 30%

7. In a lottery there are 10 prizes and 20 blanks. A ticket is chosen at random. What is the probability of not getting a prize?

   (A) $\dfrac{1}{2}$ (B) $\dfrac{2}{3}$

   (C) $\dfrac{3}{13}$ (D) $\dfrac{1}{13}$

8. From a well shuffled deck of 52 cards, one card is drawn at random. What is probability of getting a red card?

(A) $\dfrac{1}{2}$ (B) $\dfrac{1}{4}$

(C) $\dfrac{3}{13}$ (D) $\dfrac{1}{13}$

9. In a box of 100 electric bulbs, 8 bulbs are defective. One bulb is taken out at random from the box. What is the probability that the bulb drawn is not defective?

(A) $\dfrac{2}{25}$ (B) $\dfrac{1}{4}$

(C) $\dfrac{23}{25}$ (D) $\dfrac{1}{25}$

10. One card is drawn at random from a well shuffled deck of 52 cards. What is the probability that the card drawn is a queen?

(A) $\dfrac{1}{4}$ (B) $\dfrac{1}{3}$

(C) $\dfrac{1}{13}$ (D) $\dfrac{2}{13}$

11. A die is thrown. What is the probability of getting 6?

(A) 1   (B) $\dfrac{1}{2}$

(C) $\dfrac{1}{4}$ (D) $\dfrac{1}{6}$

12. From a well shuffled deck of 52 cards, one card is drawn at random. What is the probability of getting a card of black 6?

(A) $\dfrac{1}{26}$ (B) $\dfrac{1}{52}$

(C) $\dfrac{1}{13}$ (D) $\dfrac{3}{26}$

13. The ages of 50 members of the Junior cricket club in a town are as given below. 15, 17, 14, 13, 14, 13, 14, 17, 17, 16, 17, 16, 15, 16, 15, 14, 13, 14, 15, 13, 18, 13, 15, 14, 15, 13, 14, 13, 13, 17, 15, 14, 14, 17, 16, 17, 15, 14, 17, 16, 16, 16, 14, 16, 13, 18, 16, 15, 14, 14.

What percentage of members are in the 15-16 age group?

(A) 28%   (B) 30%

(C) 32%   (D) 36%

14. The pie-chart represents the amount spent on different sports by a sport club in a year. If the total money spent by the club is ₹ 10,800, find the amount spent on cricket.

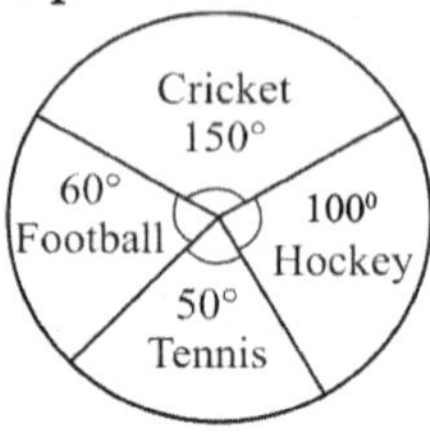

(A) 3000

(B) 4500

(C) 5000

(D) 6000

15. Mohan spends 40% of his monthly income on food items, 20% on house rent and 30% on miscellaneous items. He saves 10% of his income every month. What is the central angle for house rent on pie-chart?

(A) 144°   (B) 36°

(C) 72°   (D) 108°

16. One of letters from the word PHYSICS is chosen at random. What is the probability that this letter is S?

(A) $\dfrac{1}{7}$ (B) $\dfrac{2}{7}$

(C) $\dfrac{3}{7}$ (D) None of these

17. One of letters from the word "MOVEMENT" is chosen at random. What is the probability that this letter is M?

(A) $\dfrac{1}{2}$ (B) $\dfrac{1}{4}$

(C) $\dfrac{2}{7}$ (D) $\dfrac{1}{8}$

18. An 8-faced fair dice with numbers 1 to 8 is rolled. What is the probability of getting an even number?

(A) $\dfrac{1}{2}$ (B) $\dfrac{1}{3}$

(C) $\dfrac{1}{4}$ (D) $\dfrac{1}{6}$

19. A survey of 400 families of a town was conducted to find out how many children are there in a family?

No. of Children.	0	1	2	3	4	5
No. of family	56	82	123	95	18	26

What is the probability that a family has 3 children?

(A) $\dfrac{19}{80}$

(B) $\dfrac{19}{400}$

(C) $\dfrac{3}{95}$

(D) None of these

20. Numbers 1 to 10 are written on ten separate slips (one number on one slip), kept in a box and mixed well. One slip is chosen from the box without looking into it. What is the probability of getting a number greater than 6?

(A) $\dfrac{3}{5}$

(B) $\dfrac{2}{5}$

(C) $\dfrac{4}{7}$

(D) $\dfrac{2}{7}$

21. A bag has 4 red balls and 2 yellow balls. (The balls are identical in all respect other than colour). A ball is drawn from the bag without looking into the bag. The probability of getting a red ball is __________.

(A) 12
(B) 23
(C) 14
(D) 15

22. The histogram representing the marks obtained by 60 students in a Mathematics examination. What is the total number of students who obtained more than or equal to 80 marks in the examination?

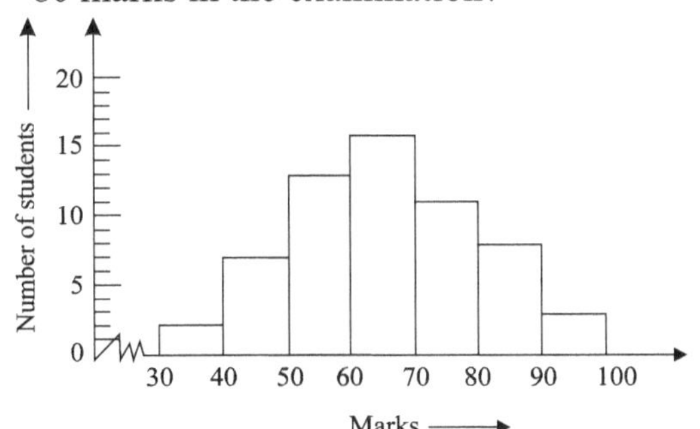

(A) 13
(B) 3

(C) 8
(D) 11

23. From the given table, the number of students who got more than or equal to 50 marks, is __________.

Marks (class-interval)	No. of students
30-40	12
40-50	13
50-60	4
60-70	15
70-80	6

(A) 15
(B) 21
(C) 25
(D) 29

24. The given pie chart gives the marks scored in an examination by a student in English, Hindi, Science and Technology, Social Science and Mathematics. If the total marks obtained by the student were 540, then the subject in which the student scored 105 marks, is__________.

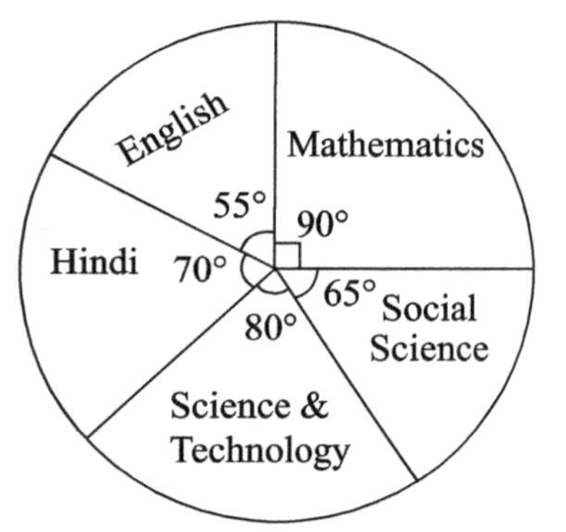

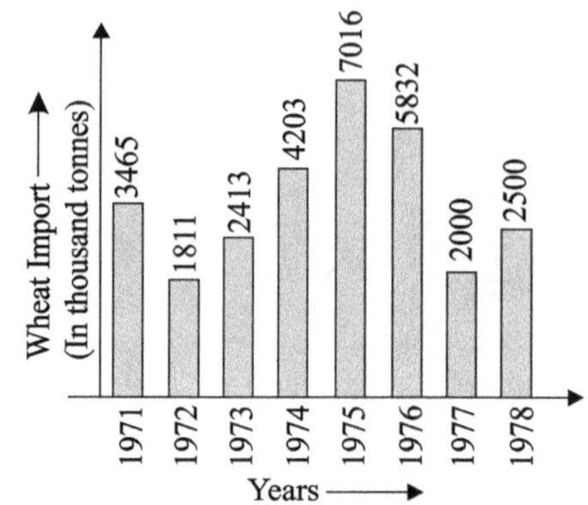

(A) English   (B) Mathematics
(C) Social Science (D) Hindi

25. Study the graph carefully and answer the questions given below it.

In which year did the wheat import register highest increase over its preceding year?

(A) 1973   (B) 1974
(C) 1975   (D) 1978

OLYMPIAD WORKBOOK (IMO) CLASS– 8

SQUARES AND SQUARE ROOTS 

LEARNING OBJECTIVES

➤ Basics of Square and Square root

MULTIPLE CHOICE QUESTIONS

1. What is the value of x if $\sqrt{\dfrac{2x-1}{3}} = 5$?

   (A) 26   (B) 28
   (C) 36   (D) 38

2. What is the greatest number of five digits which is a perfect square?
   (A) 99586   (B) 99856
   (C) 99568   (D) 99865

3. What is the least number which must be subtracted from 6459 to make it a perfect square?
   (A) 56   (B) 58
   (C) 59   (D) None of these

4. By what least number should 384 be multiplied so that the product may be a perfect square?
   (A) 2   (B) 58
   (C) 4   (D) 6

5. What is the smallest number of four digits which is a perfect square?
   (A) 1016   (B) 1024
   (C) 1036   (D) 1048

6. What is the greatest number of four digits which is a perfect square?
   (A) 9801   (B) 9816
   (C) 9824   (D) 9864

7. Find the least number which must be added to 2292 to make it a perfect square.

   (A) 10   (B) 11
   (C) 12   (D) 14

8. Find the smallest number by which 557568 must be divided so that it become a perfect square.
   (A) 2   (B) 3
   (C) 4   (D) 6

9. Find the smallest number by which 396 must be multiplied so that the product becomes a perfect square.
   (A) 3   (b)
   (C) 9   (D) 11

10. What is the least number which must be added to 6203 to obtain a perfect square ?
    (A) 32   (B) 34
    (C) 36   (D) 38

11. Find the smallest square number that is divisible by each of the number 8, 15 and 20.
    (A) 900   (B) 1600
    (C) 2500   (D) 3600

12. What is the least number that must be added to 1300 so as to get a perfect square?
    (A) 36   (B) 39
    (C) 49   (D) 69

13. What is the length of the diagonal of a square whose perimeter is equal to the perimeter of an equilateral triangle of side 4 cm?
    (A) 4. 24 cm   (B) 4.04 cm
    (C) 4.14 cm   (D) 4.64

14. The product of two positive numbers is $29\frac{31}{49}$. and one of them is three times the other. Find the larger number.

(A) $\frac{22}{7}$ (B) $\frac{66}{7}$

(C) $\frac{37}{7}$ (D) $\frac{68}{7}$

15. The area of a rectangular field whose length is three times its breadth is 348 m². What is the perimeter of the field?
(A) 82.16 m   (B) 84.16 m
(C) 86.16 m   (D) None of these

16. Which of the following is not a Pythagorean triplet?
(A) (3, 4, 5)   (B) (6, 8, 10)
(C) (2, 3, 4)   (D) (12, 35, 37)

17. The area of a square field is 60025 m². A man cycles along its boundary at 18 km/hour. In how much time will he return to the starting point?
(A) 166 seconds   (B) 176 seconds
(C) 196 Seconds   (D) None of these

18. What is the length of each side of a square whose area is equal to the area of a rectangle of length 13.6 m and breadth 3.4 meters?
(A) 4.8 m   (B) 5.8 m
(C) 6.8 m   (D) 7.8 cm

19. The perimeter of a square field is 76m. What is its area?
(A) 324 m²   (B) 289 m²
(C) 361 m²   (D) 329 m²

20. Which of the following is the square of an even number ?
(A) 729   (B) 324
(C) 441   (D) 625

HOTS (ACHIEVERS SECTION)

21. One of the factors of $x^2 + 6\sqrt{3}\,x - 48$ is $(x - 2\sqrt{3})$. What is the other factor ?

(A) $x + 8\sqrt{3}$ (B) $x - 8\sqrt{3}$

(C) $x + 6\sqrt{3}$ (D) $x - 6\sqrt{3}$

22. The square root of 0.0004 is
(A) 0.2   (B) 0.02
(C) 0.002   (D) None of these

23. What is the value of $\sqrt{\dfrac{1.21 \times 0.9}{1.1 \times 0.11}}$?

(A) 2   (B) 3
(C) 9   (D) 11

24. What is the value of $\dfrac{\sqrt{0.2401} - \sqrt{0.1681}}{\sqrt{0.2401} + \sqrt{0.1681}}$?

(A) $\frac{2}{45}$ (B) $\frac{4}{45}$

(C) $\frac{8}{45}$ (D) $\frac{16}{45}$

25. The diagonal of a square is $4\sqrt{2}$ m. What is its perimeter?
(A) 12 m
(B) 16 m
(C) 24 m
(D) None of these

———Darken Your Choice with HB Pencil———

1.	Ⓐ Ⓑ Ⓒ Ⓓ	6.	Ⓐ Ⓑ Ⓒ Ⓓ	11.	Ⓐ Ⓑ Ⓒ Ⓓ	16	Ⓐ Ⓑ Ⓒ Ⓓ	21.	Ⓐ Ⓑ Ⓒ Ⓓ
2.	Ⓐ Ⓑ Ⓒ Ⓓ	7.	Ⓐ Ⓑ Ⓒ Ⓓ	12.	Ⓐ Ⓑ Ⓒ Ⓓ	17.	Ⓐ Ⓑ Ⓒ Ⓓ	22.	Ⓐ Ⓑ Ⓒ Ⓓ
3.	Ⓐ Ⓑ Ⓒ Ⓓ	8.	Ⓐ Ⓑ Ⓒ Ⓓ	13.	Ⓐ Ⓑ Ⓒ Ⓓ	18.	Ⓐ Ⓑ Ⓒ Ⓓ	23.	Ⓐ Ⓑ Ⓒ Ⓓ
4.	Ⓐ Ⓑ Ⓒ Ⓓ	9.	Ⓐ Ⓑ Ⓒ Ⓓ	14.	Ⓐ Ⓑ Ⓒ Ⓓ	19.	Ⓐ Ⓑ Ⓒ Ⓓ	24.	Ⓐ Ⓑ Ⓒ Ⓓ
5.	Ⓐ Ⓑ Ⓒ Ⓓ	10.	Ⓐ Ⓑ Ⓒ Ⓓ	15.	Ⓐ Ⓑ Ⓒ Ⓓ	20.	Ⓐ Ⓑ Ⓒ Ⓓ	25.	Ⓐ Ⓑ Ⓒ Ⓓ

CUBES AND CUBE ROOTS

MULTIPLE CHOICE QUESTIONS

1. Simplify: $[\sqrt{12^2 + 16^2}]^3$
   (A) 400
   (B) 8000
   (C) 64000
   (D) 512000

2. Simplify: $\left(\dfrac{64}{125}\right)^{2/3}$
   (A) $\dfrac{4}{5}$
   (B) $\dfrac{8}{25}$
   (C) $\dfrac{16}{25}$
   (D) $\dfrac{4}{25}$

3. A natural number is of the form $(3n + 2)$. Its cube will be of the form:
   (A) $3n$
   (B) $3n + 1$
   (C) $3n + 2$
   (D) None of these

4. A rational number p is such that $p < 1$, then,
   (A) $p^3 > 1$
   (B) $p^3 < 0$
   (C) $p^3 < p$
   (D) $p^3 > p$

5. A real number 'p' is such that $p > 1$, then
   (A) $p^3 < 1$
   (B) $p^3 > p$
   (C) $p^3 < p$
   (D) $p^3 < 0$

6. Three numbers are in ratio $2 : 3 : 4$ and sum of their cubes is 2673. The sum of these numbers are.
   (A) 27
   (B) 26
   (C) 28
   (D) 29

7. $\left(\dfrac{4913}{343}\right)^{\frac{1}{3}} = ?$
   (A) $\dfrac{25}{7}$
   (B) $\dfrac{17}{7}$
   (C) $\dfrac{27}{7}$
   (D) $\dfrac{37}{7}$

8. Simplify: $\sqrt[3]{0.008} + \sqrt[3]{0.343} - \sqrt{0.25}$
   (A) 0.4
   (B) 0.5
   (C) 0.8
   (D) 0.7

9. Which of the following is not a perfect cube?
   (A) 2744
   (B) 704969
   (C) 513
   (D) 343

10. The length of edge of a cube whose volume is 74.088 m^3 will be
    (A) 4.52 m
    (B) 4.62 m
    (C) 4.22 m
    (D) 4.2 m

11. What is the smallest number by which 3087 may be multiplied so that the product is a perfect cube?
    (A) 2
    (B) 3
    (C) 7
    (D) None of these

12. What is the smallest number by which 8788 must be divided so that the quotient is a perfect cube?
    (A) 2
    (B) 3
    (C) 4
    (D) 6

13. What is the smallest number by which 392 may be divided so that the quotient is a perfect cube?
(A) 7
(B) 8
(C) 49
(D) None of these

14. Which of the following is a cube of odd numbers ?
(A) 2197
(B) 5129
(C) 215
(D) 1278

15. Which of the following is a cube of even numbers?
(A) 343
(B) 2197
(C) 1728
(D) 4913

16. Which of the following is a perfect cube?
(A) 441
(B) 514
(C) 412
(D) 343

17. What is the value of $\sqrt[3]{\dfrac{216}{2197}}$?
(A) $\dfrac{3}{13}$
(B) $\dfrac{6}{13}$
(C) $\dfrac{7}{13}$
(D) $\dfrac{8}{13}$

18. The value of $x^3 y^2$, if $x = 3, y = -3$ will be:
(A) 729
(B) 81
(C) 343
(D) 243

19. Find the least number which should be added to 500, to make it a perfect cube.
(A) 128
(B) 63
(C) 12
(D) 229

20. What is the least number which should be subtracted from 1370 to make the resultant, a perfect square?
(A) 29
(B) 39
(C) 49
(D) 370

HOTS (ACHIEVERS SECTION)

21. By what number should we divide 135 to get a perfect cube?
(A) 3
(B) 5
(C) 7
(D) 9

22. What should be divided by 53240 to make it a perfect cube?
(A) 5
(B) 10
(C) 15
(D) 20

23. Which of the following is a perfect cube?
(A) 125
(B) 36
(C) 75
(D) 100

24. Which of these numbers is not a cube number?
(A) 10000
(B) 343
(C) 64
(D) 729

25. When the square of a number is subtracted from the cube of the same number, it becomes 100. Find the number.
(A) 1
(B) 2
(C) 4
(D) 5

—Darken Your Choice with HB Pencil—

1.	A B C D	6.	A B C D	11.	A B C D	16	A B C D	21.	A B C D
2.	A B C D	7.	A B C D	12.	A B C D	17.	A B C D	22.	A B C D
3.	A B C D	8.	A B C D	13.	A B C D	18.	A B C D	23.	A B C D
4.	A B C D	9.	A B C D	14.	A B C D	19.	A B C D	24.	A B C D
5.	A B C D	10.	A B C D	15.	A B C D	20.	A B C D	25.	A B C D

COMPARING QUANTITIES

LEARNING OBJECTIVES

➤ Concept of Profit and Loss
➤ Discount
➤ Compound Interest

MULTIPLE CHOICE QUESTIONS

1. If 8% VAT is included in the prices, then what is the original price of a bucket bought for ₹180?
   - (A) ₹ 166.66
   - (B) ₹ 162.66
   - (C) ₹ 163.66
   - (D) ₹ 164.66

2. A milkman sold two of his cows for ₹ 20000 each. On one he made a gain of 5% and on the other a loss of 10%. What is his overall gain or loss?
   - (A) 1269.84 Loss
   - (B) 1269.84 Profit
   - (C) 1169.84 Loss
   - (D) 1169.84 Profit

3. Rahman bought a mobile for ₹ 3300 including a tax of 10%. What is the price of mobile before VAT was added?
   - (A) ₹ 2500
   - (B) ₹ 3000
   - (C) ₹ 2800
   - (D) ₹ 400

4. An article is sold at ₹ 5225 after allowing discount of 5%. What is its marked price?
   - (A) ₹ 5500
   - (B) ₹ 5400
   - (C) ₹ 5600
   - (D) ₹ 5450

5. What is the compound interest on ₹ 62500 for $1\frac{1}{2}$ years at 8% per annum compounded half yearly?
   - (A) ₹ 7804
   - (B) ₹ 7004
   - (C) ₹ 7204
   - (D) ₹ 7624

6. A scooter was bought for ₹ 42,000. Its value depreciated at the rate of 8% per annum. What is its value after one year?
   - (A) ₹ 40640
   - (B) ₹ 38,640
   - (C) ₹ 39,640
   - (D) None of these

7. By selling 20 pens a shopkeeper gains equal to the selling price of 4 pens. What is his gain percent?
   - (A) 15%
   - (B) 20%
   - (C) 25%
   - (D) 30%

8. If the S.P. of 10 articles is equal to the C.P. of 11 articles, what is the gain percent?f
   - (A) 5%
   - (B) 10%
   - (C) 15%
   - (D) 20%

9. Mohan purchased a tape recorder and spent ₹66 on its repair. He sold the tape recorder for ₹ 7130 and made a profit of 24%. At what price did he buy the tape recorder?
   - (A) ₹ 5684
   - (B) ₹ 5284
   - (C) ₹ 5784
   - (D) ₹ 5648

10. A publisher offers a discount of 10% on his books and still makes a profit of 20%. What is the actual cost of a book if it is marked at ₹ 320?
    - (A) ₹ 220
    - (B) ₹ 240
    - (C) ₹ 210
    - (D) ₹ 260

11. What is a single discount equivalent to two successive discounts of 20% and 10%?
   (A) 28%
   (B) 38%
   (C) 22%
   (D) 32%

12. In what time will ₹ 800 amount to Rs 882 at 5% per annum compounded annually?
   (A) 2 years
   (B) 2.5 years
   (C) 3 years
   (D) 4 years

13. What sum will become ₹ 9724.05 in 2 years if the rate of interest is 10% compounded half yearly?
   (A) ₹ 6000
   (B) ₹ 6800
   (C) ₹ 7200
   (D) ₹ 8000

14. What is the rate percent per annum if ₹ 2000 amount to ₹ 2662 in $1\frac{1}{2}$ years, if interest is compounded half yearly?
   (A) 20%
   (B) 10%
   (C) 25%
   (D) 16%

15. A dealer offers a discount of 20%, 10% and 5%. What is the single equivalent rate of discount?
   (A) 32.6%
   (B) 31.6%
   (C) 28.6%
   (D) 33.6%

16. The cost of a mobile phone is ₹ 3000.
   A gain of 10% should be made after a discount of 20%. What is the marked price of the mobile phone?
   (A) ₹ 4000
   (B) ₹ 4125
   (C) ₹ 4025
   (D) ₹ 4100

17. Rajesh has to pay 6% sales tax in addition to the price of a certain article. What is the price if he pays ₹ 53 to buy the article?
   (A) ₹ 45
   (B) ₹ 50
   (C) Rs 48
   (D) None of these

18. Bunti buys a leather coat costing ₹ 900 at ₹ 999, after paying the sales tax. What is rate of sales tax charged on the coat?
   (A) 10%
   (B) 9%
   (C) 11%
   (D) None of these

19. A shopkeeper increases the price of an item by 10% and then allows a discount of 15%. How much does the customer pay if the item was initially priced at ₹ 1200 ?
   (A) ₹ 1120
   (B) ₹ 1140
   (C) ₹ 1122
   (D) 1124

20. What amount will Jay receive if he deposits ₹ 8000 for 3 years at 10% per annum compounded annually?
   (A) ₹ 10228
   (B) ₹ 10348
   (C) ₹ 10548
   (D) ₹ 10648

21. A businessman marks his goods at 40% above the cost price and allows a discount of 25%. What is his gain percent?
   (A) 5%
   (B) 10%
   (C) 15%
   (D) 20%

22. The cost price of 12 books is equal to selling price of 15 books. What is the loss percent?
   (A) 10%
   (B) 20%
   (C) 15%
   (D) 25%

23. Calculate the compound interest on ₹ 10000 at 10% per annum for 3 years, if interest is compounded annually?
   (A) ₹ 3130
   (B) ₹ 1331
   (C) ₹ 3310
   (D) ₹ 13310

24. The value of a machine depreciates at the rate of 20% per annum. It was purchased 2 years ago if its present value is ₹ 4000, for how much was it purchased?
   (A) ₹ 6250
   (B) ₹ 6280
   (C) ₹ 6520
   (D) ₹ 5650

25. If the simple interest on a sum of money at 5% per annum for 3 years is ₹ 1200, then what is the compound interest on the same sum for the same period at the same rate?
   (A) ₹ 1261
   (B) ₹ 1225
   (C) ₹ 1241
   (D) ₹ 1251

26. The difference between the S.I. and C.I. on ₹ 2500 for 2 years at 20% when the compound interest is payable annually is
    (A) ₹ 50
    (B) ₹ 70
    (C) ₹ 100
    (D) ₹ 200

27. In what time will ₹ 64,000 amount to ₹ 68921 at 5% per annum if interest payable is compounded half yearly?
    (A) 1.5 years
    (B) 2.5 years
    (C) 2 years
    (D) 3.5 years

28. A mobile set is sold for ₹ 1498 and the seller gains 7% on it. What is its cost price?
    (A) 1200
    (B) 1400
    (C) 1440
    (D) 1460

29. The cost of the article was ₹ 15500 and ₹ 500 was spent on its repairing. If it is sold for a profit of 15%. The selling price of the article is:
    (A) ₹16400
    (B) ₹17400
    (C) ₹18400
    (D) ₹19400

30. Two bicycles were sold for ₹ 3990 each, gaining 5% on one and losing 5% on the other. The gain or loss percent on the whole transaction is
    (A) Neither gain nor loss
    (B) 2.5% gain
    (C) 2.5% loss
    (D) 0.25% loss

ALGEBRAIC EXPRESSIONS AND THEIR IDENTITIES

9

LEARNING OBJECTIVES

➤ Algebraic Expressions
➤ Operations on Algebraic Expression
➤ Factorisation of Algebraic Expressions

MULTIPLE CHOICE QUESTIONS

1. If $x + y = 12$ and $xy = 14$ then what is the value of $x^2 + y^2$?
   (A) 116 (B) 114
   (C) 112 (D) 118

2. If $x + \dfrac{1}{x} = 11$ then what is the value of $x^2 + \dfrac{1}{x^2}$?
   (A) 123 (B) 119
   (C) 117 (D) 121

3. If $x + y = 10$ and $xy = 9$, what is the value of $x^2 - y^2$?
   (A) 40 (B) 60
   (C) 80 (D) 90

4. If $x + \dfrac{1}{x} = 7$ then find the value of $x^4 + \dfrac{1}{x^4}$.
   (A) 2209 (B) 2207
   (C) 2211 (D) 2205

5. The perimeter of a triangle is $6m^2 - 4m + 9$ and two of the sides are $m^2 - 2m + 1$ and $2m^2 + 3m + 5$. What is the third side?
   (A) $3m^2 - 5m + 3$
   (B) $3m^2 + 5m - 3$
   (C) $5m^2 - 3m + 3$
   (D) $5m^2 - 3m + 3$

6. What is the remainder when $7 + 15\,x - 13x^2 + 5x^3$ is divided by $4 - 3x + x^2$?
   (A) $x - 1$ (B) $x + 1$
   (C) $1 - x$ (D) None of these

7. What is the quotient if $x^4 - 2x^3 + 2x^2 + x + 4$ is divided by $x^2 + x + 1$?
   (A) $x^2 - 3x + 4$ (B) $x^2 - 3x + 2$
   (C) $x^2 + 3x - 4$ (D) None of these

8. What is the quotient if $5x^3 - 4x^2 + 3x + 18$ is divided by $3 - 2x + x^2$?
   (A) $5x - 6$ (B) $5x + 6$
   (C) $6x - 5$ (D) $6x + 5$

9. If $x - \dfrac{1}{x} = 6$ then what is the value of $x^2 + \dfrac{1}{x^2}$?
   (A) 38 (B) 36
   (C) 34 (D) None of these

10. $8\,a^2 b^3 \div (-2ab)$?
    (A) $4\,a^2b$ (B) $-4ab^2$
    (C) $-4a^2b$ (D) $4\,ab^2$

11. What is the value of $\dfrac{198 \times 198 - 102 \times 102}{96}$?
    (A) 200 (B) 300
    (C) 400 (D) None of these

12. What is the numerical coefficient in the product of $2abc$, $-16a^2bc$ and $3ab^2c^2$?
   (A) 64   (B) 96
   (C) −96   (D) −64

13. If $x+\dfrac{1}{x}=2$, what is the value of $x^4+\dfrac{1}{x^4}$?
   (A) 4   (B) 2
   (C) 1   (D) None of these

14. What is the value of $\dfrac{8.37\times8.37-1.63\times1.63}{0.674}$?
   (A) 10   (B) 100
   (C) 1000   (D) None of these

15. What is the remainder when $6x^2-11x+15$ is divided by $2x-5$?
   (A) 15   (B) 25
   (C) 35   (D) −25

16. What is the quotient if $15p^4+16p^3+\dfrac{10p}{3}-9p^2-6$ is divided by $3p-2$?

   (A) $5p^3+\dfrac{26}{9}p^2+\dfrac{25}{8}p+\dfrac{80}{27}$

   (B) $5p^3+\dfrac{16}{3}p^2+\dfrac{15}{9}p+\dfrac{80}{27}$

   (C) $5p^3+\dfrac{26}{9}p^2+\dfrac{25}{3}p+\dfrac{80}{27}$

   (D) $5p^1+\dfrac{26}{3}p^2+\dfrac{25}{9}p+\dfrac{80}{27}$

17. What is the H.C.F. of $11\,abc^3$, $13\,a^2b^2c$ and $17\,ab^3c^2$?
   (A) abc (B) ab^2c
   (C) a^2bc (D) $3abc$

18. If one of the factors of $x^2-y^2+2yz-x^2z^2$ is $(x+y-z)$ then what is the other factor?
   (A) $(x+y-z)$ (B) $(x-y+z)$
   (C) $(x+y+z)$ (D) $(x-y-z)$

19. If one of the factors of x^4+x2+1 is (x^2+x+1) then what is the other factor?
   (A) x^2-x+1 (B) x^2+x-1
   (C) x^2+x+1 (D) None of these

20. What are the factors of $11a^2+54a+63$?
   (A) $(11a+21)(a+3)$
   (B) $(11a+21)(a-3)$
   (C) $(11a+9)(a+7)$
   (D) $(11a+7)(a+9)$

21. What is the degree of the polynomial?
   $1-\dfrac{5}{3}x+9x^2-6x^3-x^4$?
   (A) 1   (B) 2
   (C) 3   (D) 4

22. Find the remainder when x^4+4x^2+10 is divided by x^2-2x+4.
   (A) −6   (B) 6
   (C) 4   (D) −4

23. Which of the following is not a polynomial ?
   (A) x^2-x+1 (B) $x^2+\sqrt{x}-2$
   (C) x^3-x2-1 (D) x^4-x+3

24. Find the product:
   $\dfrac{1}{4}x^2\,y^2z^2\times3x\times\dfrac{3}{2}y^2z$?

   (A) $\dfrac{3}{4}x^3\,y^2\,z^2$ (B) $\dfrac{3}{4}x^3\,y^3\,z^3$

   (C) $\dfrac{9}{8}x^3\,y^4\,z^3$ (D) $\dfrac{9}{8}x^3\,y^4\,z^2$

25. If $\left(x-\dfrac{1}{x}\right)^2=36$ then what is the value of $x^4+\dfrac{1}{x^4}$?
   (A) 1442   (B) 1440
   (C) 1444   (D) 1438

26. What is the value of x if
$$\frac{(x+3)(7-2x)}{(x+4)(5-x)} = 2$$

   (A) 17   (B) -17

   (C) 19   (D) -19

27. $9x^2 + 25 - 30x$ is the square of

   (A) $3x - 5$

   (B) $-3x - 5$

   (C) $3x + 5$

   (D) $-3x^2 + 5$

28. One of the factors of $x^2 + 17x + 60$ is

   (A) $x + 12$ (B) $x - 5$

   (C) $5x - 1$ (D) $x - 12$

29. If we add, $7xy + 5yz - 3zx$, $4yz + 9zx - 4y$ and $-3xz + 5x - 2xy$, then the answer is:

   (A) $5xy + 9yz + 3zx + 5x - 4y$

   (B) $5xy - 9yz + 3zx - 5x - 4y$

   (C) $5xy + 10yz + 3zx + 15x - 4y$

   (D) $5xy + 10yz + 3zx + 5x - 6y$

30. If we subtract $4a - 7ab + 3b + 12$ from $12a - 9ab + 5b - 3$, then the answer is:

   (A) $8a+2ab+2b+15$

   (B) $8a+2ab+2b-15$

   (C) $8a-2ab+2b-15$

   (D) $8a-2ab-2b-15$

1.	Ⓐ Ⓑ Ⓒ Ⓓ	7.	Ⓐ Ⓑ Ⓒ Ⓓ	13.	Ⓐ Ⓑ Ⓒ Ⓓ	19	Ⓐ Ⓑ Ⓒ Ⓓ	25.	Ⓐ Ⓑ Ⓒ Ⓓ
2.	Ⓐ Ⓑ Ⓒ Ⓓ	8.	Ⓐ Ⓑ Ⓒ Ⓓ	14.	Ⓐ Ⓑ Ⓒ Ⓓ	20.	Ⓐ Ⓑ Ⓒ Ⓓ	26.	Ⓐ Ⓑ Ⓒ Ⓓ
3.	Ⓐ Ⓑ Ⓒ Ⓓ	9.	Ⓐ Ⓑ Ⓒ Ⓓ	15.	Ⓐ Ⓑ Ⓒ Ⓓ	21.	Ⓐ Ⓑ Ⓒ Ⓓ	27.	Ⓐ Ⓑ Ⓒ Ⓓ
4.	Ⓐ Ⓑ Ⓒ Ⓓ	10.	Ⓐ Ⓑ Ⓒ Ⓓ	16.	Ⓐ Ⓑ Ⓒ Ⓓ	22.	Ⓐ Ⓑ Ⓒ Ⓓ	28.	Ⓐ Ⓑ Ⓒ Ⓓ
5.	Ⓐ Ⓑ Ⓒ Ⓓ	11.	Ⓐ Ⓑ Ⓒ Ⓓ	17.	Ⓐ Ⓑ Ⓒ Ⓓ	23.	Ⓐ Ⓑ Ⓒ Ⓓ	29.	Ⓐ Ⓑ Ⓒ Ⓓ
6.	Ⓐ Ⓑ Ⓒ Ⓓ	12.	Ⓐ Ⓑ Ⓒ Ⓓ	18.	Ⓐ Ⓑ Ⓒ Ⓓ	24.	Ⓐ Ⓑ Ⓒ Ⓓ	30.	Ⓐ Ⓑ Ⓒ Ⓓ

VISUALISING SOLID SHAPES  10

MULTIPLE CHOICE QUESTIONS

1. A polyhedron such that its base and top are congruent polygons and other faces (lateral) are parallelograms in shape will be a
   (A) Pyramid   (B) Cylinder
   (C) Prism   (D) Tetrahedron

2. A regular polyhedron has :
   (A) Congruent faces
   (B) Non-congruent faces
   (C) Vertices are formed by different number of faces
   (D) None of these

3. A cylinder has :
   (A) 2 surfaces   (B) 3 surfaces
   (C) 4 surfaces   (D) 5 surfaces

4. A tetrahedron has :
   (A) 3 equilateral triangles
   (B) 4 equilateral triangles
   (C) 5 equilateral triangles
   (D) 4 isosceles triangles

5. A hexahedron has :
   (A) 8 squares
   (B) 6 squares
   (C) 6 rectangles
   (D) 6 parallelograms

6. A paraboloid is formed by :
   (A) Extruding a parabola.
   (B) Rotating a parabola about its vertex.
   (C) Rotating a parabola about its axis.
   (D) None of these.

7. The number of edges of a octahedron are :
   (A) 16   (B) 17
   (C) 18   (D) 20

8. A dodecahedron has 12 regular
   (A) Equilateral triangles
   (B) Pentagons
   (C) Squares
   (D) Rectangles

9. The number of faces of an icosahedron are :
   (A) 14
   (B) 16
   (C) 18
   (D) 20

10. A solid is formed by rotating right-angled triangle about any of its altitudes. The solid will be :
    (A) Cylinder (Right circular)
    (B) Sphere
    (C) Cone (Right Circular)
    (D) Hemisphere

11. If two equal tetrahedrons are joined through their base triangles, by sticking, then the shape generated will be a :
   (A) Tetrahedron
   (B) Hexahedron
   (C) Dodecahedron
   (D) Decahedron

12. While drawing an isometric view of a cube, the sides should be inclined at :
   (A) $30°$ to the horizontal
   (B) $30°$ to the vertical
   (C) $(30° + 30°) = 60°$, to the vertical
   (D) both (a) and (c)

13. The front view of a tetrahedron will be :

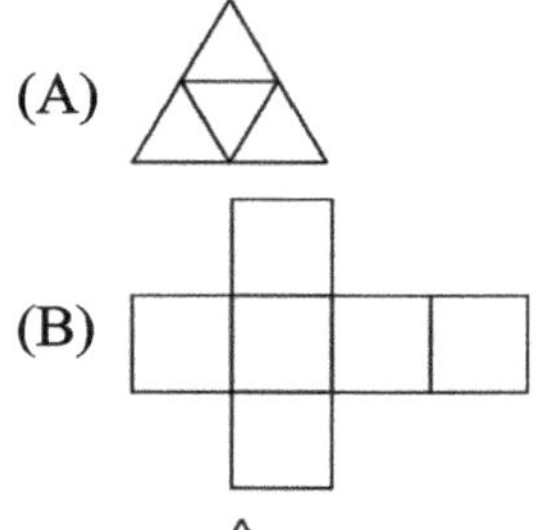

   (A)

   (B)

   (C)

   (D) None of these

14. 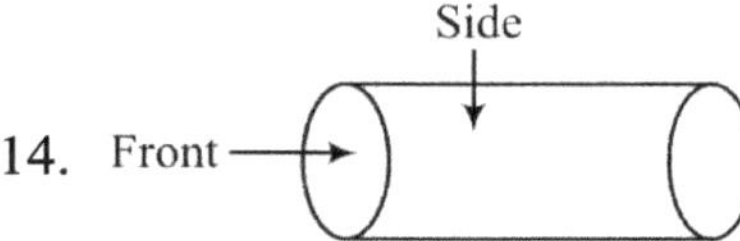

   The front and side views of a right circular cylinder are :
   (A) Circular, Triangular
   (B) Circular, Rectangular
   (C) Curved, straight
   (D) None of these.

15. A solid shape is generated by rotating a rectangle about any of its sides. The shape will be :
   (A) Cuboid
   (B) Cone
   (C) Sphere
   (D) Cylinder (right circular)

16. A solid shape is generated by extruding a rectangle, out of its plane. The shape will be :
   (A) Cube   (B) Cuboid
   (C) Cylinder   (D) Cone

17. The top view will contain :

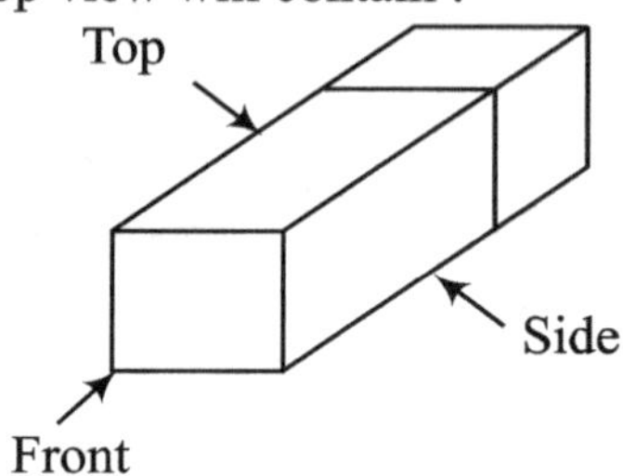

   (A) 1 rectangle, 1 square (joined)
   (B) 2 squares (joined)
   (C) 2 rectangles (joined)
   (D) 1 rectangle.

18. 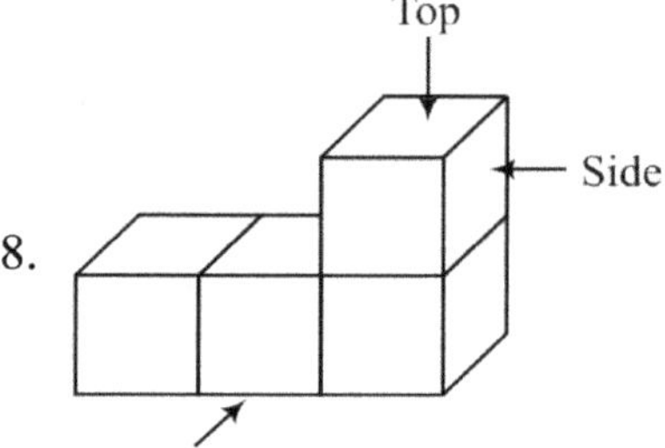

   The above figure is generated from 4 cubes; The number of squares in front view $= x$, number of squares in top view $= y$ then $(x + y) =$
   (A) 7   (B) 6
   (C) 5   (D) 8

19. 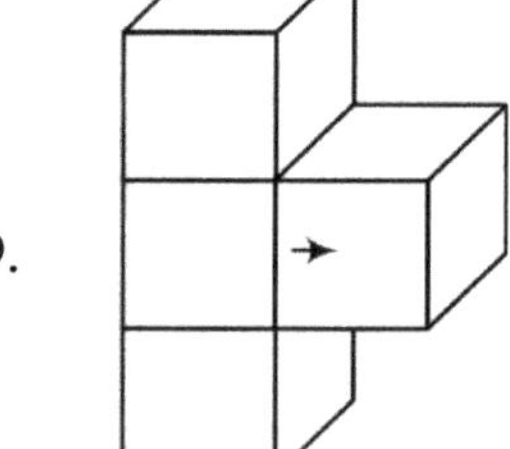

   A cube is extracted from a well-arranged vertical cubes, which are 3 in number. When viewed from top, the number of edges will be :
   (A) 8   (B) 6
   (C) 7   (D) 10

20. 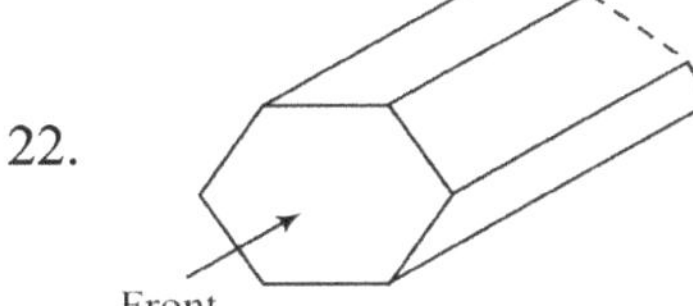

The above solid contain 3 cubes. The number of edges will be : (cubes are of same dimensions)

(A) 30   (B) 32

(C) 28   (D) 36

21. Number of vertices in Q – 25 are : (cubes are of same dimension)

(A) 24   (B) 12

(C) 18   (D) 20

22.

The front view of the given shape will have _____ edges.

(A) 5   (B) 6

(C) 7   (D) 4

23. 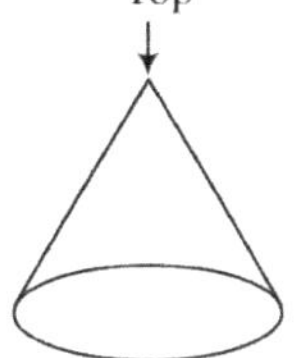

The top view of a cone will be :

(A) Square   (B) Rectangular

(C) Triangle   (D) Circular

24. A parallelogram is extruded outwards with the axis inclined at some angle with the vertical. The resulting figure will be :

(A) Cuboid   (B) Parallelopiped

(C) Parallelex   (D) None of these.

25. 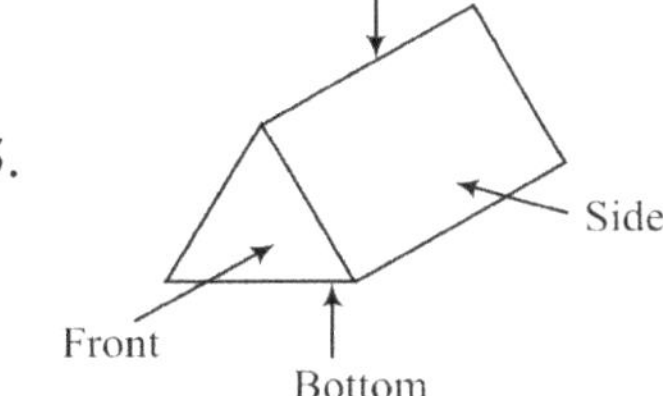

The number of vertices in front view + number of vertices in top view - number of vertices in bottom view =

(A) 4   (B) 6

(C) 5   (D) 9

HOTS (ACHIEVERS SECTION)

26. A solid is of the shape given. Which is its top view?

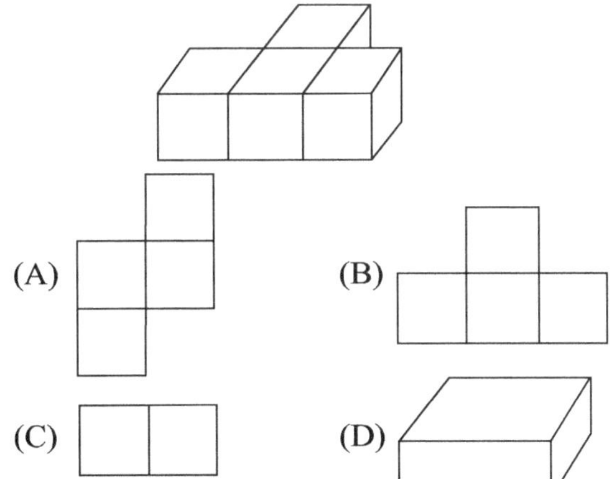

(A)   (B)

(C)   (D)

27. Observe the following solid.

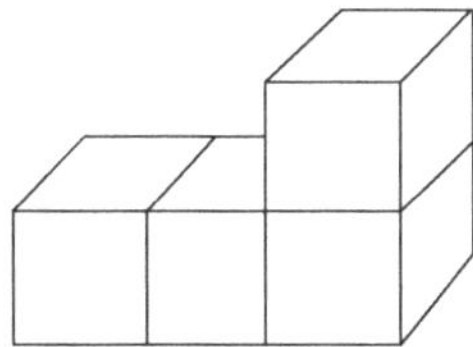

The following box has a figure which is a view of the given solid.

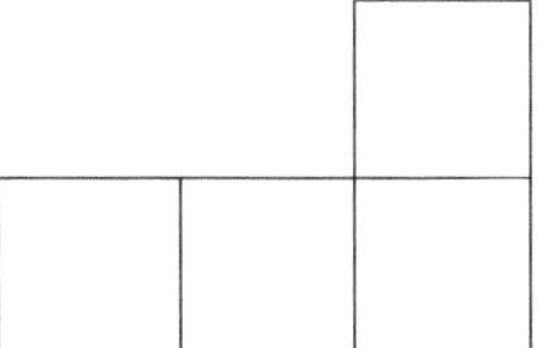

Which view of the solid is shown in the box?
(A) Side view   (B) Top view
(C) Back view   (D) Front view

28. Which one of the following cubes can be formed by the net given?

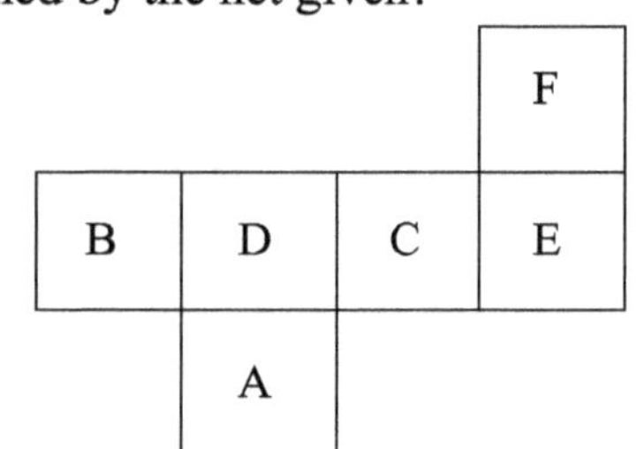

(A) 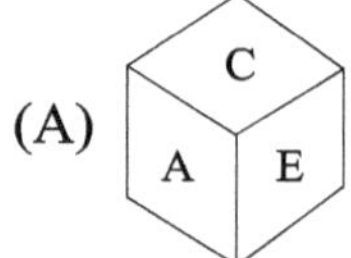
(B) 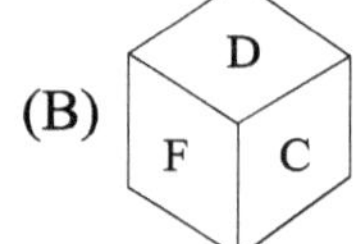
(C) 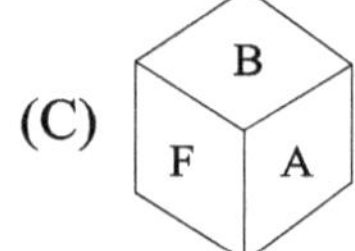
(D) 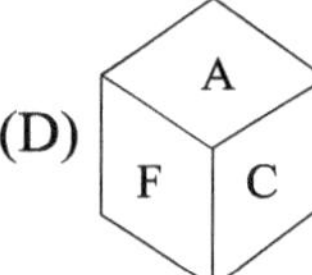

29. If two cubes of dimensions 3 cm × 3 cm × 3 cm are placed side by side, what would the dimensions of the resulting cuboid be?

(A) 6 cm × 6 cm × 6 cm

(B) 12 cm ×12 cm × 12 cm

(C) 9 cm × 6 cm × 3 cm

(D) 6 cm × 3 cm × 3 cm

30. How many triangles can be seen in this figure?

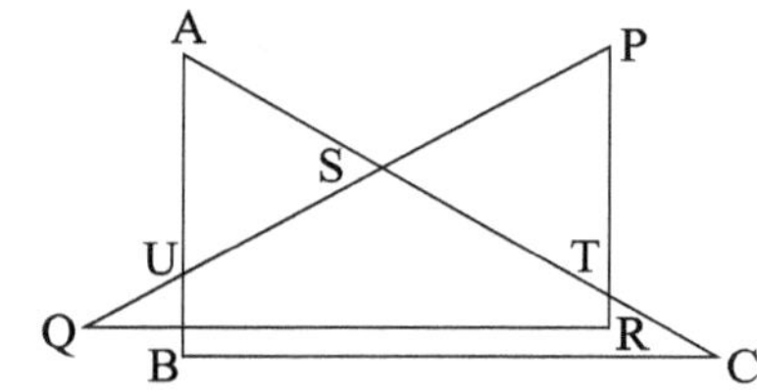

(A) 5

(B) 8

(C) 10

(D) 11

MENSURATION

LEARNING OBJECTIVES

➤ Basics of Mensuration

MULTIPLE CHOICE QUESTIONS

1. A cylindrical tank has capacity of 5632 m³. Its diameter is 16 m. What is its depth?
   (A) 24 m (B) 26 m
   (C) 28 m (D) 32 m

2. The volume of a cylinder of height 8 cm is 1232 cm³. What is the difference between its curved surface area and total surface area?
   (A) 352 cm² (B) 308 cm²
   (C) 316 cm² (D) 332 cm²

3. What is the volume of a cube whose total surface area is 486 cm² ?
   (A) 729 cm³ (B) 572 cm³
   (C) 343 cm³ (D) None of these

4. A beam of wood is 5 m long and 36 cm thick. It is made of 1.35 m³ of wood. What is the width of the beam?
   (A) 15 cm (B) 25 cm
   (C) 75 cm (D) None of these

5. How many planks of size 2m × 25 cm × 8 cm can be prepared from a wooden block 5 m long 70 cm broad and 32 cm thick ?
   (A) 28 (B) 32
   (C) 36 (D) 42

6. The radius and height of a cylinder are in the ratio 3 : 7. Its volume is 1584 cu cm. What is the radius of the cylinder?
   (A) 2 cm (B) 4 cm
   (C) 6 cm (D) 8 cm

7. How many bricks of size 22 cm × 10 cm × 7 cm are required to construct a wall 33 m long 3.5 m high and 40 cm thick and sand used in the construction occupy $\frac{1}{10}$ th part of the wall?
   (A) 24000 (B) 25000
   (C) 26000 (D) 27000

8. A rectangular sheet of paper 44 cm × 18 cm is rolled along its length and a cylinder is formed. What is the volume of that cylinder?
   (A) 2772 cm³ (B) 2722 cm³
   (C) 2727 cm³ (D) 2277 cm³

9. The area of the base of a cone is 180 cm². If the height of the cone is 8 cm what is its volume?
   (A) 420 cm³ (B) 480 cm³
   (C) 460 cm³ (D) 520 cm³

10. The radii of two cylinders are in the ratio 2 : 3 and their heights are in the ratio 5 : 3. What is the ratio of their volumes?
    (A) 20 : 27 (B) 27 : 20
    (C) 10 : 9 (D) 9 : 10

11. A swimming pool is 260 m long and 140 m wide. If 54600 cubic metres of water is pumped into it, what is the height of the water level in it ?
    (A) 1 m (B) 1·5 m
    (C) 2 m (D) 2·5 m

12. A rectangular piece of paper 22 cm × 6 cm is folded without overlapping to make a cylinder of height 6 cm. What is the volume of the cylinder?

(A) 221 cm³ (B) 231 cm³
(C) 214 cm³ (D) 243 cm³

13. The lateral surface area of a cylinder is 11440 cm³. If its height is 65 cm then what is its circumference?

(A) 174 cm (B) 176 cm
(C) 184 cm (D) 186 cm

14. In the given figure the outer dimension is 24 cm × 28 cm and the inner dimension 16 cm × 20 cm. What is the difference between two adjacent section of the frame if the width of each section is same?

(A) 20 cm²
(B) 24 cm²
(C) 16 cm²
(D) 28 cm

15. The area of a trapezium is 480 m². The distance between two parallel sides is 15 m and one of the parallel side is 20 m. What is the length of other parallel side?

(A) 42 m (B) 44 m
(C) 48 m (D) 52 m

16. A rectangular piece of paper 11 cm × 4 cm is folded without overlapping to make a cylinder of height 4 cm. What is its volume?

(A) 32·5 cm³
(B) 36·5 cm³
(C) 38·5 cm³
(D) None of these

17. The total surface area of a cube is 486 m². Then what is the measure of its side?

(A) 7 cm (B) 8 cm
(C) 9 cm (D) 12 cm

18. The parallel sides of a trapezium are 25 cm and 11 cm and its non-parallel sides are 15 cm and 13 cm. What is the area of trapezium?

(A) 216 cm² (B) 242 cm²
(C) 226 cm² (D) 256 cm²

19. The area of a trapezium is 384 cm². Its parallel sides are in the ratio 5 : 3 and the distance between them is 12 cm. What is the length of longer of the parallel sides?

(A) 36 cm (B) 40 cm
(C) 42 cm (D) 44 cm

20. In the given figure $ST = SR$, $PQ = QR = RT = TP = 25$ m and its 5 total height is 41 m. What is its total area?

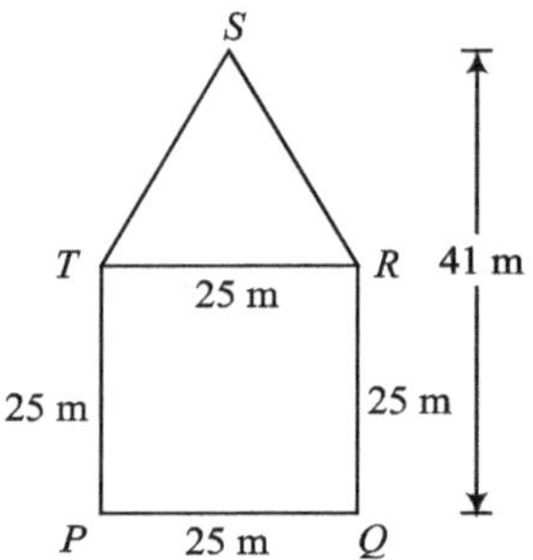

(A) 825 m²
(B) 815 m²
(C) 845 m²
(D) None of these

21. $ABCD$ is a quadrilateral field in which the diagonal BD is 36 m. $AL \perp BD$ and $CM \perp BD$ such that $AL = 19$ m and $CM = 11$ m. What is the area of the field?

(A) 520 m²
(B) 540 m²
(C) 560 m²
(D) 570 m²

22. If the length of each side of a cube is doubled then by how many times does its surface area increase?

(A) 4 times
(B) 8 times
(C) 16 times
(D) None of these

23. The edges of a cuboid are in the ratio 1 : 2 : 3 and its surface area is 88 cm². What is the volume of the cuboid?

(A) 48 cm³ (B) 64 cm³
(C) 56 cm³ (D) 64 cm³

OLYMPIAD WORKBOOK (IMO) CLASS– 8

24. The curved surface area of a cylinder is 220 cm² and then volume of the cylinder is 770 cm³ then what is the diameter of cylinder?

(A) 7 cm   (B) 14 cm

(C) 21 cm   (D) 28 cm

25. The circumference of the circular base of a cylinder is 44 cm and its height is 15 cm. What is the volume of the cylinder?

(A) 1155 cm³   (B) 1540 cm³

(C) 2310 cm³   (D) None of these

HOTS (ACHIEVERS SECTION)

26. The area of the base of a cone is 180 cm². If the height of the cone is 8 cm what is its volume?

(A) 480 cm³   (B) 1440 cm³

(C) 6188 cm³   (D) 22.5 cm³

27. The curved surface area of a cylinder is 5940 cm². If its height is 30 cm, what is the diameter of the base?

(A) 36 cm   (B) 198 cm

(C) 31.5 cm   (D) 63 cm

28. A cuboid vessel is 20 cm long and 12 cm wide. How high must it be to hold 3 liters of water?

(A) 12.5 cm   (B) 12 cm

(C) 14 cm   (D) 4.5 cm

29. The perimeter of a rectangle is 54 cm. If its width is 2 cm more than one-fourth of its length, what is its length?

(A) 12 cm   (B) 16 cm

(C) 20 cm   (D) 24 cm

30. A well with internal diameter 8m is dug 7m deep. The earth taken out of it is spread around to a width of 2 m to form an embankment. The height of embankment will be :

(A) 1.4 m   (B) 2.8 m

(C) 4.2 m   (D) 5.6 m

—Darken Your Choice with HB Pencil—

1.	Ⓐ Ⓑ Ⓒ Ⓓ	7.	Ⓐ Ⓑ Ⓒ Ⓓ	13.	Ⓐ Ⓑ Ⓒ Ⓓ	19	Ⓐ Ⓑ Ⓒ Ⓓ	25.	Ⓐ Ⓑ Ⓒ Ⓓ
2.	Ⓐ Ⓑ Ⓒ Ⓓ	8.	Ⓐ Ⓑ Ⓒ Ⓓ	14.	Ⓐ Ⓑ Ⓒ Ⓓ	20.	Ⓐ Ⓑ Ⓒ Ⓓ	26.	Ⓐ Ⓑ Ⓒ Ⓓ
3.	Ⓐ Ⓑ Ⓒ Ⓓ	9.	Ⓐ Ⓑ Ⓒ Ⓓ	15.	Ⓐ Ⓑ Ⓒ Ⓓ	21.	Ⓐ Ⓑ Ⓒ Ⓓ	27.	Ⓐ Ⓑ Ⓒ Ⓓ
4.	Ⓐ Ⓑ Ⓒ Ⓓ	10.	Ⓐ Ⓑ Ⓒ Ⓓ	16.	Ⓐ Ⓑ Ⓒ Ⓓ	22.	Ⓐ Ⓑ Ⓒ Ⓓ	28.	Ⓐ Ⓑ Ⓒ Ⓓ
5.	Ⓐ Ⓑ Ⓒ Ⓓ	11.	Ⓐ Ⓑ Ⓒ Ⓓ	17.	Ⓐ Ⓑ Ⓒ Ⓓ	23.	Ⓐ Ⓑ Ⓒ Ⓓ	29.	Ⓐ Ⓑ Ⓒ Ⓓ
6.	Ⓐ Ⓑ Ⓒ Ⓓ	12.	Ⓐ Ⓑ Ⓒ Ⓓ	18.	Ⓐ Ⓑ Ⓒ Ⓓ	24.	Ⓐ Ⓑ Ⓒ Ⓓ	30.	Ⓐ Ⓑ Ⓒ Ⓓ

EXPONENTS AND POWERS

LEARNING OBJECTIVES

➤ Powers and exponents

MULTIPLE CHOICE QUESTIONS

1. What is the value of $(4^{-1} + 8^{-1}) \div \left(\dfrac{2}{3}\right)^{-1}$?

    (A) $\dfrac{3}{2}$ (B) $\dfrac{1}{4}$

    (C) $\dfrac{1}{8}$ (D) $\dfrac{1}{16}$

2. What is the value of $\left(\dfrac{1}{2}\right)^{-3} + \left(\dfrac{1}{3}\right)^{-3} + \left(\dfrac{1}{4}\right)^{-3}$?

    (A) 27   (B) 25

    (C) 99   (D) 87

3. By what number should $\left(\dfrac{1}{2}\right)^{-1}$ be multiplied so that the product is $\left(\dfrac{-5}{4}\right)^{-1}$?

    (A) $\dfrac{2}{5}$ (B) $\dfrac{-2}{5}$

    (C) $\dfrac{1}{5}$ (D) $\dfrac{-1}{5}$

4. By what number should $(-6)^{-1}$ be multiplied so that the product becomes 9^{-1}?

    (A) $\dfrac{-1}{3}$ (B) $\dfrac{2}{3}$

    (C) $\dfrac{-2}{3}$ (D) $\dfrac{1}{3}$

5. What is the standard form of 0.00000000837?

    (A) 8.37×10^9 (B) 8.37×10^{-9}

    (C) 83.7×10^{-8} (D) 837×10^{-7}

6. What is the value of x for which.

    $$\left(\dfrac{7}{12}\right)^{-4} \times \left(\dfrac{7}{12}\right)^{3x} = \left(\dfrac{7}{12}\right)^{5} ?$$

    (A) -1 (B) 1

    (C) 2   (D) 3

7. The value of $(3^{-1} + 4^{-1})^{-1} \div 5^{-1} = ?$

    (A) $\dfrac{7}{10}$ (B) $\dfrac{7}{15}$

    (C) $\dfrac{7}{5}$ (D) $\dfrac{60}{7}$

8. If $(2^{3x-1} + 10) \div 7 = 6$ then what is the value of x?

    (A) 0   (B) 1

    (C) -2 (D) 2

9. What is the usual form of 0.000467×10^4?

    (A) 4.67   (B) 46.7

    (C) 0.467   (D) 0.0467

10. If $\left(\dfrac{5}{4}\right)^{-2} \div \left(\dfrac{-5}{4}\right)^{-3} = \left(\dfrac{-4}{5}\right)^{x}$, find x?

    (A) -1 (B) 1

    (C) 2   (D) -2

11. What will be the value of $\left[(2)^{\frac{1}{2}}\right]^{4x}$, where $x = -0.5$?

(A) 2   (B) $\dfrac{1}{4}$

(C) $\dfrac{1}{2}$ (D) 4

12. Express 1 micron in standard form.

(A) $\dfrac{1}{100000}$ m   (B) 1×10^{-6} m

(C) $\dfrac{1}{10000}$ m   (D) 1×10^{-5} m

13. The value of $(5^{-3} + 5^{-2} + 5^{-1} + 5^0)$ is :
(A) 5^{-4} (B) 2.248
(C) 1.248   (D) 3.248

14. If $5^2 p + 5p + 5^0 = 651$, then $p =$
(A) 2   (B) 3
(C) 4   (D) 5

15. If $\dfrac{5^3}{5^2} \div \dfrac{3^5}{2^5} \times \dfrac{2^x}{3^x} = 0.0578$, then $x =$

(A) 2   (B) 3
(C) 4   (D) 6

16. $(32)^{2x+1} = (8)^{-x} (4)^{-4}$, the value of x will be:
(A) 1   (B) -1
(C) 2   (D) -2

17. By what number should $(23)^{-3}$ be multiplied with so that the product becomes $(69)^{-1}$?

(A) $\dfrac{529}{4}$ (C) $\dfrac{529}{7}$

(C) $\dfrac{529}{3}$ (D) $\dfrac{529}{6}$

18. $(5^{-1} + 6^{-1}) \div 22 = k^{-1}$, then k will be equal to:
(A) 20   (B) 30
(C) 40   (D) 60

19. The distance between earth and the sun is 15×10^7 km. Express this distance in metres.
(A) 15×10^{11} m   (B) 1.5×10^9 m
(C) 1.5×10^{11} m   (D) 1.5×10^8 m

20. Simplify :

$$\left(\dfrac{25}{16}\right)^4 \div \left(\dfrac{225}{144}\right)^{-3}$$

(A) $\left(\dfrac{5}{4}\right)^2$ (B) $\left(\dfrac{5}{4}\right)^{14}$

(C) $\left(\dfrac{5}{4}\right)^{12}$ (D) $\left(\dfrac{5}{4}\right)^3$

21. $(6+3) \times 9^{-1} \div 3^{-1} + 2^{-2} =$

(A) $\dfrac{5}{4}$ (B) $\dfrac{7}{4}$

(C) $\dfrac{13}{4}$ (D) $\dfrac{7}{8}$

22. Find the value of $\dfrac{p^m}{p^n} \times \dfrac{n^p}{m^p} \div \dfrac{m^{p+n}}{p^{n+m}} =$ if $m \neq 0, p \neq 0$ and $m = n = p$.
(A) 1   (B) p^{2p}
(C) $p^{2p} + 1$ (D) p^{3p}

23. The size of a plant cell is 0.00001275 m. Express this measure in standard form.
(A) 1275×10^{-6} (B) 1275×10^{-5} m
(C) 1.275×10^{-5} (D) 1.275×10^{-6} m

24. $\left[\left(\dfrac{1}{3}\right)^{-2} - \left(\dfrac{1}{4}\right)^{-2}\right]^{-2} \times 7^2 =$

(A) 49   (B) 0
(C) 7   (D) 1

25. $2^{3x+5} \times 3^{2x+5} = (6)^{3x+2}$, then $3^x =$
(A) 6   (B) 52
(C) 144   (D) 216

26. In 10 days earth picks up 2.6×10^8 kg of dust from the atmosphere. How much dust will it pick up in 45 days?

    (A) 1.17×10^9 kg

    (B) 1.17×10^7 kg

    (C) 1.17×10^5 kg

    (D) 1.17×10^4 kg

27. What is the value of $\dfrac{x^0 - y^0}{x^0 + y^0}$?

    (A) 0   (B) 1

    (C) 2   (D) -1

28. If $(-3)^{m+1} \times (-3)^5 = (-3)^7$, then the value of m is:

    (A) 5   (B) 7

    (C) 1   (D) 3

29. 1.8×1011 is equal to:

    (A) 180000000000

    (B) 18000000000

    (C) 1800000000

    (D) 1800000000000

30. 0.09×10^{10} is equal to:

    (A) 900000000   (B) 9000000

    (C) 9000   (D) 9

—Darken Your Choice with HB Pencil—

1.	(A) (B) (C) (D)	7.	(A) (B) (C) (D)	13.	(A) (B) (C) (D)	19	(A) (B) (C) (D)	25.	(A) (B) (C) (D)
2.	(A) (B) (C) (D)	8.	(A) (B) (C) (D)	14.	(A) (B) (C) (D)	20.	(A) (B) (C) (D)	26.	(A) (B) (C) (D)
3.	(A) (B) (C) (D)	9.	(A) (B) (C) (D)	15.	(A) (B) (C) (D)	21.	(A) (B) (C) (D)	27.	(A) (B) (C) (D)
4.	(A) (B) (C) (D)	10.	(A) (B) (C) (D)	16.	(A) (B) (C) (D)	22.	(A) (B) (C) (D)	28.	(A) (B) (C) (D)
5.	(A) (B) (C) (D)	11.	(A) (B) (C) (D)	17.	(A) (B) (C) (D)	23.	(A) (B) (C) (D)	29.	(A) (B) (C) (D)
6.	(A) (B) (C) (D)	12.	(A) (B) (C) (D)	18.	(A) (B) (C) (D)	24.	(A) (B) (C) (D)	30.	(A) (B) (C) (D)

DIRECT AND INVERSE VARIATIONS

LEARNING OBJECTIVES

➤ Direct Variation and related concepts

MULTIPLE CHOICE QUESTIONS

1. A train is running at 36 km/hour. If it crosses a pole in 25 seconds, then what is its length?
   (A) 250 m (B) 225 m
   (C) 275 m (D) 300 m

2. A garrison of 1500 men had provision for 38 days. However a reinforcement of 400 men arrived. For how many days will the provision last?
   (A) 28 days (B) 30 days
   (C) 32 days (D) 34 days

3. Manish can pack 260 bundles in 5 days. How many bundles can he pack in 7 days?
   (A) 264 (B) 364
   (C) 384 (D) 324

4. A worker is paid ₹ 280 for 8 days work. If the total income of the month was ₹ 945, for how many days did he work?
   (A) 25 days (B) 26 days
   (C) 27 days (D) 28 days

5. A bus is travelling at an average speed of 56 km/hour. How much distance will it travel in 15 minutes?
   (A) 14 km (B) 12 km
   (C) 13 km (D) 16 km

6. In 15 days, the earth picks up 1.2×10^8 kg of dust from the atmosphere. In how many days will it pick up 4.8×10^8 kg of dust?
   (A) 40 days (B) 50 days
   (C) 30 days (D) 60 days

7. Suppose L and M vary inversely. When L is 10, M is 6. Which of the following is not a possible pair of corresponding values of L and M?
   (A) 12 and 5 (B) 15 and 4
   (C) 45 and 1.3 (D) 25 and 2.4

8. If 28 people can do a piece of work in 65 days, how many people can do it in 35 days?
   (A) 48 (B) 46
   (C) 52 (D) 56

9. A 270 m long train is running at 81 km/hr. How much time will it take to cross a 225 m long platform?
   (A) 18 sec (B) 21 sec
   (C) 22 sec (D) 24 sec

10. By working 8 hours a day Ankur can copy a book in 18 days. How many hours a day should he work so as to finish the work in 12 days?
    (A) 10 hours (B) 12 hours
    (C) 14 hours (D) 16 hours

11. If 6 men can do a job in 8 days, in how many days can 8 men do it?
    (A) 4 days (B) 5 days
    (C) 6 days (D) 8 days

12. A factory requires 42 machines to produce a given number of articles in 56 days. How many machines would be required to produce the same number of articles in 48 days?
    (A) 40 (B) 46
    (C) 48 (D) 49

13. A photograph of a bacteria enlarged 70000 times attains a length of 7 cm. What is the actual length of the bacteria?
(A) 10^3 cm
(B) 10^{-3} cm
(C) 10^{-2} cm
(D) 10^{-4} cm

14. If 5 men or 7 women can earn ₹ 1372 per day, how much would 10 men and 5 women earn per day?
(A) ₹ 3724
(B) ₹ 3624
(C) ₹ 3524
(D) ₹ 3124

15. 11 people can dig $6\dfrac{3}{4}$ m long trench in one day. How many men should be employed for digging 27 m trench of the same type in one day?
(A) 42 men
(B) 43 men
(C) 44 men
(D) 46 men

16. The scale of a map is $1:3 \times 10^7$. Two cities are 5cm apart on the map. What is the actual distance between them in kilometer ?
(A) 1000 km
(B) 1200 km
(C) 1500 km
(D) None of these

17. A loaded truck covers 18 km in 35 minutes. At the same speed how far can it travel in 7 hours?
(A) 196 km
(B) 216 km
(C) 212 km
(D) 192 km

18. 6 cows can graze a field in 28 days. How long would 21 cows take to graze the same field?
(A) 6 days
(B) 8 days
(C) 7 days
(D) 12 days

19. A car is travelling at a uniform speed of 84 km/hr. How much distance will it cover in 15 minutes?
(A) 16 km
(B) 18 km
(C) 19 km
(D) 21 km

20. Ranjna types 510 words in half an hour. How many words would she type in 10 minutes?
(A) 153
(B) 150
(C) 170
(D) 85

HOTS (ACHIEVERS SECTION)

21. If the weight of 12 sheets of thick paper is 40 grams, how many sheets of the same paper would weigh 2500 grams?
(A) 750
(B) 800
(C) 850
(D) 950

22. The scale of a map is given as 1:300. Two cities are 4 km apart on the map. The actual distance between them is:
(A) 1000 km
(B) 1100 km
(C) 1200 km
(D) 1300 km

23. 6 pipes are required to fill a tank in 1 hour 20 minutes. If we use 5 such types of pipes, how much time it will take to fill the tank?
(A) 120 minutes
(B) 96 minutes
(C) 80 minutes
(D) 85 minutes

24. A man walks 20 km in 5 hours. How much time it will take for him to walk 32 km?
(A) 3 hours
(B) 4 hours
(C) 6 hours
(D) 8 hours

25. If 300 kg of coal cost 6000`, then find the cost of 120 kg of coal?
(A) ₹1200
(B) ₹2400
(C) ₹3200
(D) ₹4200

———Darken Your Choice with HB Pencil———

1.	Ⓐ Ⓑ Ⓒ Ⓓ	6.	Ⓐ Ⓑ Ⓒ Ⓓ	11.	Ⓐ Ⓑ Ⓒ Ⓓ	16	Ⓐ Ⓑ Ⓒ Ⓓ	21.	Ⓐ Ⓑ Ⓒ Ⓓ
2.	Ⓐ Ⓑ Ⓒ Ⓓ	7.	Ⓐ Ⓑ Ⓒ Ⓓ	12.	Ⓐ Ⓑ Ⓒ Ⓓ	17.	Ⓐ Ⓑ Ⓒ Ⓓ	22.	Ⓐ Ⓑ Ⓒ Ⓓ
3.	Ⓐ Ⓑ Ⓒ Ⓓ	8.	Ⓐ Ⓑ Ⓒ Ⓓ	13.	Ⓐ Ⓑ Ⓒ Ⓓ	18.	Ⓐ Ⓑ Ⓒ Ⓓ	23.	Ⓐ Ⓑ Ⓒ Ⓓ
4.	Ⓐ Ⓑ Ⓒ Ⓓ	9.	Ⓐ Ⓑ Ⓒ Ⓓ	14.	Ⓐ Ⓑ Ⓒ Ⓓ	19.	Ⓐ Ⓑ Ⓒ Ⓓ	24.	Ⓐ Ⓑ Ⓒ Ⓓ
5.	Ⓐ Ⓑ Ⓒ Ⓓ	10.	Ⓐ Ⓑ Ⓒ Ⓓ	15.	Ⓐ Ⓑ Ⓒ Ⓓ	20.	Ⓐ Ⓑ Ⓒ Ⓓ	25.	Ⓐ Ⓑ Ⓒ Ⓓ

FACTORISATION

➤ Degree of the Polynomials

MULTIPLE CHOICE QUESTIONS

1. The factorisation of $12a^2b+15ab^2$ gives:
   (A) $3ab(4ab + 5)$　　(B) $3ab(4a + 5b)$
   (C) $3a(4a + 5b)$　　(D) $3b(4a + 5b)$

2. The factorisation of $12x + 36$ is
   (A) $12(x + 3)$　　(B) $12(3x)$
   (C) $12(3x + 1)$　　(D) $x(12 + 36x)$

3. On factorising $14pq + 35pqr$, we get:
   (A) $pq(14 + 35r)$
   (B) $p(14q + 35qr)$
   (C) $q(14p + 35pr)$
   (D) $7pq(2 + 5r)$

4. The factors of $6xy - 4y + 6 - 9x$ are:
   (A) $(3x + 2)(2y + 3)$
   (B) $(3x - 2)(2y - 3)$
   (C) $(3x - 2)(2y + 3)$
   (D) $(3x - +2)(2y - 3)$

5. The factors of $x^2 + xy + 8x + 8y$ are:
   (A) $(x + y)(x + 8)$
   (B) $(2x + y)(x + 8)$
   (C) $(x + 2y)(x + 8)$
   (D) $(x + y)(2x + 8)$

6. The factors of $4y^2 - 12y + 9$ is:
   (A) $(2y + 3)^2$
   (B) $(2y - 3)^2$
   (C) $(2y - 3)(2y + 3)$
   (D) None of the above

7. The factors of $49p^2 - 36$ are:
   (A) $(7p + 6)^2$
   (B) $(7p - 6)^2$
   (C) $(7p - 6)(7p + 6)$
   (D) None of the above

8. The factors of $m^2 - 256$ are:
   (A) $(m + 4)^2$
   (B) $(m - 4)^2$
   (C) $(m - 4)(m + 4)$
   (D) None of the above

9. When we factorise $x^2 + 5x + 6$, then we get:
   (A) $(x +2)(x + 3)$　　(B) $(x - 2)(x - 3)$
   (C) $(x \times 2) + (x \times 3)$　　(D) $(x \times 2) - (x \times 3)$

10. The factors of $3m^2 + 9m + 6$ are:
    (A) $(m + 1)(m + 2)$　　(B) $3(m + 1)(m + 2)$
    (C) $6(m + 1)(m + 2)$　　(D) $9(m + 1)(m + 2)$

11. The common factor of a^3b^3 and ab^2 is:
    (A) a^2b^2　　(B) ab^2
    (C) a^2b　　(D) ab

12. The common factor of a^3b^2 and a^4b is:
    (A) a^4b^2　　(B) a^4b
    (C) a^3b^2　　(D) a^3b

13. The common factor $12a$ and 30 is:
    (A) 6　　(B) 12
    (C) 30　　(D) $6a$

14. The common factors of $10a$, $20b$ and $30c$ are:
   (A) ab (B) ac
   (C) $10abc$ (D) 10

15. The common factor of $6x^3y^4z^2$, $21x^2y$ and $15x^3$ is:
   (A) $3x^2$ (B) $3x^3$
   (C) $6x^3$ (D) $6x^2$

16. The common factor of $24a^3b^4$, $36a^4c^4$ and $48a^3b^2c$ is:
   (A) $12a^3$ (B) $24a3$
   (C) $36a^3$ (D) $48a3$

17. The factorisation of $12x^2y + 15xy^2$ is:
   (A) $3xy^2(4x + 5y)$
   (B) $3x^2y(4x + 5y)$
   (C) $3xy(4x + 5y)$
   (D) $3x^2y^2(4x + 5x)$

18. The factorisation of $5x - 20$ is:
   (A) $5(x - 5)$ (B) $5(x - 4)$
   (C) $5(x - 3)$ (D) $5(x - 20)$

19. The factorisation of $8x + 4y$ is:
   (A) $8(x + 4y)$ (B) $4(2x + 4y)$
   (C) $8(x + y)$ (D) $4(2x + y)$

20. The factors of xyz are:
   (A) x
   (B) y
   (C) z
   (D) All of the above

HOTS (ACHIEVERS SECTION)

21. Which of the following is the common factor of $25a^2b$ and $55ab^2$?
   (A) $5ab^2$ (B) $5a^2b$
   (C) $5ab$ (D) $5a^2b^2$

22. The common factor of $6a^2b4c^2$, $21a^2b$ and $15a^3$ is
   (A) $3a^3$ (B) $6a^3$
   (C) $6a^2$ (D) $3a^2$

23. The factorisation of $12a^2b + 15ab^2$ is
   (A) $3ab(4a + 5b)$
   (B) $3a^2b(4a + 5b)$
   (C) $3ab^2(4a + 5b)$
   (D) $3a^2b^2(4a + 5b)$

24. The factorisation of $10x^2 - 18x^3 + 14x^4$ is
   (A) $2x^3(7x^2 - 9x + 5)$
   (B) $2x(7x^2 - 9x + 5)$
   (C) $2x^2(7x^2 - 9x + 5)$
   (D) $2(7x^2 - 9x + 5)$

25. The value of $3.5 \times 3.5 - 2.5 \times 2.5$ is
   (A) -6 (B) 6
   (C) 60 (D) 1

1.	Ⓐ Ⓑ Ⓒ Ⓓ	6.	Ⓐ Ⓑ Ⓒ Ⓓ	11.	Ⓐ Ⓑ Ⓒ Ⓓ	16	Ⓐ Ⓑ Ⓒ Ⓓ	21.	Ⓐ Ⓑ Ⓒ Ⓓ
2.	Ⓐ Ⓑ Ⓒ Ⓓ	7.	Ⓐ Ⓑ Ⓒ Ⓓ	12.	Ⓐ Ⓑ Ⓒ Ⓓ	17.	Ⓐ Ⓑ Ⓒ Ⓓ	22.	Ⓐ Ⓑ Ⓒ Ⓓ
3.	Ⓐ Ⓑ Ⓒ Ⓓ	8.	Ⓐ Ⓑ Ⓒ Ⓓ	13.	Ⓐ Ⓑ Ⓒ Ⓓ	18.	Ⓐ Ⓑ Ⓒ Ⓓ	23.	Ⓐ Ⓑ Ⓒ Ⓓ
4.	Ⓐ Ⓑ Ⓒ Ⓓ	9.	Ⓐ Ⓑ Ⓒ Ⓓ	14.	Ⓐ Ⓑ Ⓒ Ⓓ	19.	Ⓐ Ⓑ Ⓒ Ⓓ	24.	Ⓐ Ⓑ Ⓒ Ⓓ
5.	Ⓐ Ⓑ Ⓒ Ⓓ	10.	Ⓐ Ⓑ Ⓒ Ⓓ	15.	Ⓐ Ⓑ Ⓒ Ⓓ	20.	Ⓐ Ⓑ Ⓒ Ⓓ	25.	Ⓐ Ⓑ Ⓒ Ⓓ

INTRODUCTION TO GRAPHS

LEARNING OBJECTIVES

➤ Basics of bar diagrams and pie charts
➤ Different types of graphs
➤ Advantages and disadvantages of various graphs

MULTIPLE CHOICE QUESTIONS

1. A __________ is a bar graph that shows data in intervals.
   - (A) Bar-graph
   - (B) Pie-chart
   - (C) Histograph
   - (D) Line Graph

2. A graph that displays data that changes continuously over periods of time is called:
   - (A) Bar-graph
   - (B) Pie-chart
   - (C) Histograph
   - (D) Line Graph

3. A line graph which is a whole unbroken line is called a:
   - (A) Linear graph
   - (B) Pie-chart
   - (C) Histograph
   - (D) Bar-graph

4. Which point lies only on y-axis?
   - (A) $(-2, 0)$
   - (B) $(2, 0)$
   - (C) $(0, -2)$
   - (D) $(2, -2)$

5. If we join $(-3, 2)$, $(-3, -3)$ and $(-3, 4)$, then we obtain:
   - (A) A triangle
   - (B) Straight-line without passing through origin
   - (C) Straight-line passing through origin
   - (D) None of the above

6. The point $(4, 0)$ lies on which of the following?
   - (A) x-axis
   - (B) y-axis
   - (C) origin
   - (D) None of the above

7. The point $(-2, -2)$ is:
   - (A) near to x-axis
   - (B) near to y-axis
   - (C) near to origin
   - (D) Equidistant from x-axis and y-axis.

8. The point $(-2, 5)$ is nearer to:
   - (A) x-axis
   - (B) y-axis
   - (C) origin
   - (D) None of the above

9. The point $(-5, 2)$ is nearer to:
   - (A) x-axis
   - (B) y-axis
   - (C) origin
   - (D) None of the above

10. The point $(0, 0)$ lies at:
    - (A) x-axis
    - (B) y-axis
    - (C) origin
    - (D) None of the above

Observe the diagram, given below and find the correct answer to the following MCQs.

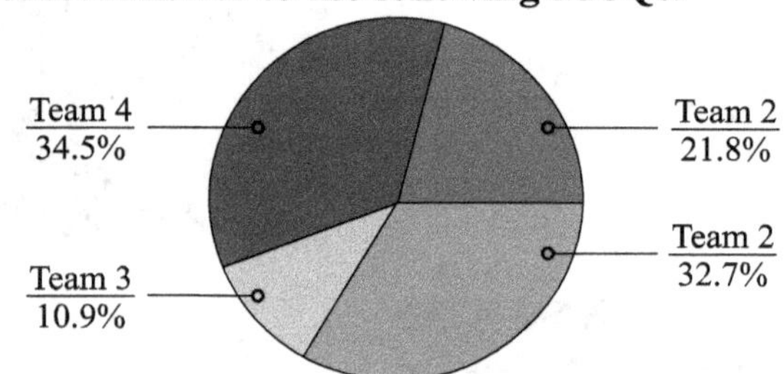

11. Which team has the highest score?
    (A) Team 1
    (B) Team 2
    (C) Team 3
    (D) Team 4

12. Which team has the lowest score?
    (A) Team 1
    (B) Team 2
    (C) Team 3
    (D) Team 4

13. Which team is coloured green?
    (A) Team 1   (B) Team 2
    (C) Team 3   (D) Team 4

14. What is the average score of all the teams?
    (A) 22%   (B) 25%
    (C) 27%   (D) 29%

15. Which team has the second-highest score?
    (A) Team 1
    (B) Team 2
    (C) Team 3
    (D) Team 4

    Below is the data of the number of men and women in a village for different years. Now based on this data answer the following MCQs with the correct option.

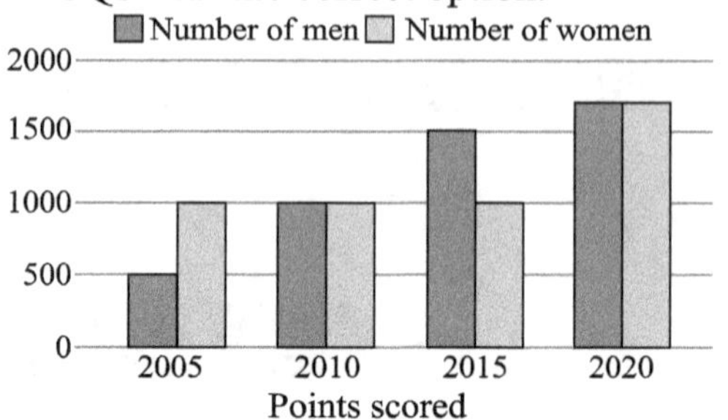

16. How many men were there in the village in 2010?
    (A) 500
    (B) 1000
    (C) 1500
    (D) 2000

17. The population of men and women in 2020 is the same?
    (A) True   (B) False

18. In which year the population of women is the highest?
    (A) 2005
    (B) 2010
    (C) 2015
    (D) 2020

19. When is the population of men, the minimum?
    (A) 2005
    (B) 2010
    (C) 2015
    (D) 2020

20. In which year population of men is more than women?
    (A) 2005   (B) 2010
    (C) 2015   (D) 2020

21. Which of the following points lies on y-axis?
    (A) (–4, 0) (B) (4, 0)
    (C) (0, –4) (D) (–4, 4)

22. By joining (–3, 2) (–3, 3) and (–3, 4), which of the following is obtained?
    (A) Triangle
    (B) A straight line not passing through origin
    (C) A straight line passing through origin.
    (D) None of these

23. By joining (1, 1), (0, 0) and (3, 3), which of the following is obtained?
    (A) A triangle
    (B) A straight line passing through origin
    (C) A curved line
    (D) A straight line not passing through origin

24. **DIRECTION:** The following graph shows the temperature of a patient admitted in a hospital, recorded every 2 hours.

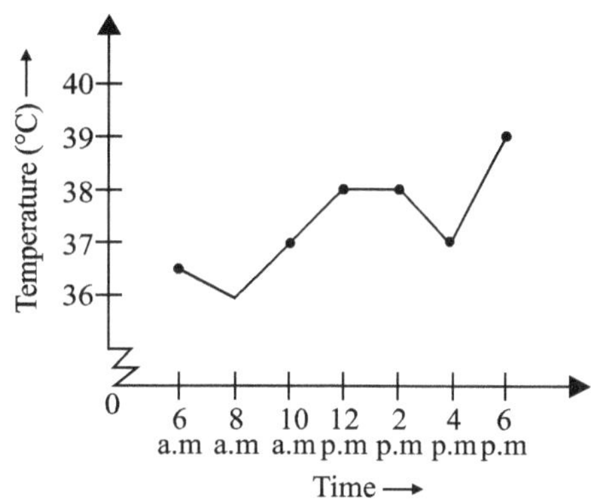

What was the patient's temperature at 3 p.m.?
    (A) 37.5°C (B) 38°C
    (C) 36°C (D) 37°C

25. Based on above graph, when was the patient's temperature highest?
    (A) 10 a.m. (B) 6 p.m.
    (C) 4 p.m. (D) 2 p.m.

Darken Your Choice with HB Pencil

1. Ⓐ Ⓑ Ⓒ Ⓓ	6. Ⓐ Ⓑ Ⓒ Ⓓ	11. Ⓐ Ⓑ Ⓒ Ⓓ	16 Ⓐ Ⓑ Ⓒ Ⓓ	21. Ⓐ Ⓑ Ⓒ Ⓓ
2. Ⓐ Ⓑ Ⓒ Ⓓ	7. Ⓐ Ⓑ Ⓒ Ⓓ	12. Ⓐ Ⓑ Ⓒ Ⓓ	17. Ⓐ Ⓑ Ⓒ Ⓓ	22. Ⓐ Ⓑ Ⓒ Ⓓ
3. Ⓐ Ⓑ Ⓒ Ⓓ	8. Ⓐ Ⓑ Ⓒ Ⓓ	13. Ⓐ Ⓑ Ⓒ Ⓓ	18. Ⓐ Ⓑ Ⓒ Ⓓ	23. Ⓐ Ⓑ Ⓒ Ⓓ
4. Ⓐ Ⓑ Ⓒ Ⓓ	9. Ⓐ Ⓑ Ⓒ Ⓓ	14. Ⓐ Ⓑ Ⓒ Ⓓ	19. Ⓐ Ⓑ Ⓒ Ⓓ	24. Ⓐ Ⓑ Ⓒ Ⓓ
5. Ⓐ Ⓑ Ⓒ Ⓓ	10. Ⓐ Ⓑ Ⓒ Ⓓ	15. Ⓐ Ⓑ Ⓒ Ⓓ	20. Ⓐ Ⓑ Ⓒ Ⓓ	25. Ⓐ Ⓑ Ⓒ Ⓓ

PLAYING WITH NUMBERS

LEARNING OBJECTIVES

- ➤ Numbers in general form
- ➤ Letters for Digit
- ➤ Tests of Divisibility

MULTIPLE CHOICE QUESTIONS

1. $\begin{array}{r} 1\,8\,2 \\ \times 2\,2 \\ \hline a\,0\,0\,a \end{array}$, the value of 'a' will be:

    (A) 2   (B) 3
    (C) 4   (D) 8

2. What will be the last digit of 7^{333} ?

    (A) 1   (B) 7
    (C) 3   (D) 9

3. Which of the following numbers is divisible by 11?

    (A) 1221   (B) 1223
    (C) 1332   (D) 1343

4. $\begin{array}{r} 7\,3\,x\,5 \\ -\,2\,y\,7\,7 \\ \hline 4\,5\,1\,8 \end{array}$, the value of $(x + y)$ will be:

    (A) 16   (B) 17
    (C) 18   (D) 15

5. $\begin{array}{r} a\,a \\ \times a\,a \\ \hline b\,8\,b \end{array}$, Given $1 \le a, b \le 9$

    then the value of (ab) will be:

    (A) 32   (B) 16
    (C) 8   (D) 4

6. 763*312, which number should the * be replaced with to make the number divisible by 9?

    (A) 7   (B) 5
    (C) 8   (D) 6

7. 76215*, if the replacement of * by a number gives a number which is divisible by 11, the number will be:

    (A) 8   (B) 7
    (C) 6   (D) 9

8. $\begin{array}{r} A\,B\,C \\ A\,B\,C \\ +\,A\,B\,C \\ \hline B\,B\,B \end{array}$, the values of A, B, C are digits from 1 to 9. What will be value of B?

    (A) 8   (B) 4
    (C) 1   (D) 3

9. What will be the sum of first 22 even natural numbers?

    (A) 506   (B) 406
    (C) 484   (D) 253

10. One candle was guaranteed to burn for 6 hours, the other for 2 hours. They were both lit at same time. After some time one candle was twice as long as the other. For how long had they been burning?

(A) 3 hours   (B) $\dfrac{6}{5}$ hours

(C) $\dfrac{4}{3}$ hours   (D) $\dfrac{3}{2}$ hours

11. Find a 3-digit number, such that all its digits are prime and the 3 digits are the factors of the number?

(A) 735   (B) 537
(C) 435 9   (D) 245

12. Complete the square given below and find the value of the sum of missing numbers. The sum of the magic square is 34.

5	x	e	d
16	y	7	c
a	13	b	6
2	z	9	f

(A) 68   (B) 39
(C) 78   (D) 84

13. Three numbers are such that their sum is 10 and their product is maximum. The product will be:

(A) 32   (B) 36
(C) 45   (D) 42

14. What will be the one's place digit of 6^{222}?

(A) 4   (B) 8
(C) 1   (D) 6

15. Find the smallest number which can be expressed as the sum of two cubes of natural numbers.

(A) 1729   (B) 1001
(C) 1728   (D) 1332

16. $\dfrac{\begin{array}{r} P\,A\,T \\ +\,E\,A\,T \end{array}}{F\,E\,E\,A}$, where, P, A, T, E, F are digits from 1 to 9 what will be the value of F?

(A) 4   (B) 3
(C) 2   (D) 1

17. Sum of 3 numbers = product of these 3 numbers. If the numbers are consecutive and natural, find the triplet having least value for their sum.

(A) 2, 3, 4
(B) 1, 2, 3
(C) 3, 4, 6
(D) 1, – 1, 0

18. The square of a number is having 5 at its units place and 2 at its tenths place, then the least natural number having these properties are:

(A) 5   (B) 15
(C) 25   (D) 4

19. The product 135×135 will be equal to:

(A) 19625   (B) 16925
(C) 18225   (D) 16235

20. Which of the following number is not a perfect square?

(A) 1024
(B) 441
(C) 1681
(D) 1282

HOTS (ACHIEVERS SECTION)

21. Umesh tossed a coin three times. What is the probability that Umesh gets more heads than tails?

(A) 0.5
(B) 0.125
(C) 0.375
(D) None of these

22. If 28 men can do a piece of work in 65 days, how many men can do it in 35 days?

(A) 48 men   (B) 52 men
(C) 56 men   (D) 62 men

23. The sum of digits of a two-digit number is 9. If 9 is subtracted from the number, its digits are interchanged. What is the half of that number?

(A) 26   (B) 27
(C) 28   (D) 29

24. The product of two numbers is 1575 and their quotient is $\dfrac{9}{7}$. What is the difference between the numbers?

(A) 5

(B) 10

(C) 15

(D) 20

25. Suppose A is a digit. Find the value of A if $31A + 1A3 = 501$.

(A) 1

(B) 2

(C) 3

(D) 4

1.	Ⓐ Ⓑ Ⓒ Ⓓ	6.	Ⓐ Ⓑ Ⓒ Ⓓ	11.	Ⓐ Ⓑ Ⓒ Ⓓ	16	Ⓐ Ⓑ Ⓒ Ⓓ	21.	Ⓐ Ⓑ Ⓒ Ⓓ
2.	Ⓐ Ⓑ Ⓒ Ⓓ	7.	Ⓐ Ⓑ Ⓒ Ⓓ	12.	Ⓐ Ⓑ Ⓒ Ⓓ	17.	Ⓐ Ⓑ Ⓒ Ⓓ	22.	Ⓐ Ⓑ Ⓒ Ⓓ
3.	Ⓐ Ⓑ Ⓒ Ⓓ	8.	Ⓐ Ⓑ Ⓒ Ⓓ	13.	Ⓐ Ⓑ Ⓒ Ⓓ	18.	Ⓐ Ⓑ Ⓒ Ⓓ	23.	Ⓐ Ⓑ Ⓒ Ⓓ
4.	Ⓐ Ⓑ Ⓒ Ⓓ	9.	Ⓐ Ⓑ Ⓒ Ⓓ	14.	Ⓐ Ⓑ Ⓒ Ⓓ	19.	Ⓐ Ⓑ Ⓒ Ⓓ	24.	Ⓐ Ⓑ Ⓒ Ⓓ
5.	Ⓐ Ⓑ Ⓒ Ⓓ	10.	Ⓐ Ⓑ Ⓒ Ⓓ	15.	Ⓐ Ⓑ Ⓒ Ⓓ	20.	Ⓐ Ⓑ Ⓒ Ⓓ	25.	Ⓐ Ⓑ Ⓒ Ⓓ

LOGICAL REASONING

LEARNING OBJECTIVES

- ➤ Alphabet Order
- ➤ Solving questions related to Odd one out
- ➤ Letter Coding
- ➤ Solving questions related to direction sense test
- ➤ Solving questions related to series completion
- ➤ Solving questions related to pattern
- ➤ Solving questions related to number ranking
- ➤ Solving questions related to analytical reasoning
- ➤ Solving questions related to Venn diagram

MULTIPLE CHOICE QUESTIONS

1. If ZOO stands for 56, DEER stands for 32 then for which numerical value does LION stand for?
   - (A) 48
   - (B) 49
   - (C) 50
   - (D) 51

2. If JEANS = 49, COAT = 39 then SHIRT = ?
   - (A) (a) 71
   - (B) 72
   - (C) 73
   - (D) 74

3. If BUD = 27, ROSE = 57 then FLOWER = ?
   - (A) 77
   - (B) 78
   - (C) 79
   - (D) 80

   Direction : Choose the odd one from the given group.

4. (A) Spanner   (B) Shovel
   (C) Spade   (D) Rave

5. (A) Harbour   (B) Island
   (C) Coast   (D) Oasis

6. (A) Fibula   (B) Appendix
   (C) Pelvis   (D) Vertebra

7. In a certain code, HAND is written as SZMW, then what will be the code of MILK?
   - (A) NROP
   - (B) NOPR
   - (C) NORP
   - (D) RNOP

8. In a certain code TURN is written as VWTP, then how is WALK written in that code?
   - (A) VCMN
   - (B) YCNM
   - (C) YBMN
   - (D) YCON

9. In a coding language GUAVA is coded as HVBWB, then how is JUICE written in that language ?
   - (A) KVHEF
   - (B) KVJDF
   - (C) KVIEG
   - (D) KUJDT

10. Nitesh faces towards North. Turning to his right he walks 20 meters. He then turns to his left and walks 20 meters, then he moves 30 m to his right then turns to his right again and walks 45 meters. At last he turns to his right and moves 35 meters. In which direction is he now from the starting position?
    - (A) South
    - (B) South-East
    - (C) South-West
    - (D) North-East

11. Ranjan is looking for Ratan. He went 90m towards the East before turning to his right. He went 20m before turning to his right again to look, for Ratan at Mohan's position 30m from this point. Ratan was not there. From that point he went 100m to his North before

meeting Ratan. What is the shortest distance between Ranjan's starting point and Ratan's position?

(A) 60 m   (B) 80 m
(C) 100 m   (D) 120 m

12. Dinesh walks 10m towords East and 10m to the right then turning to his left three times he walks 5m, 15m, 15 m respectively. How far is he from his starting position?

(A) 5 m   (B) 10 m
(C) 15 m   (D) None of these

Direction: Find the next term in the following series.

13. 6, 15, 28, 45, 66, ...?

(A) 91   (B) 92
(C) 93   (D) 94

14. 12, 19, 28, 39, 52,?

(A) 65   (B) 66
(C) 67   (D)

15. 10, 22, 46, 94, ?

(A) 189   (B) 190
(C) 191   (D) 192

16. 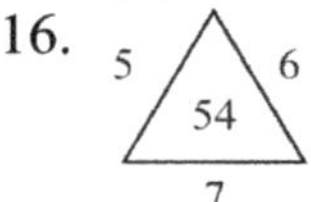 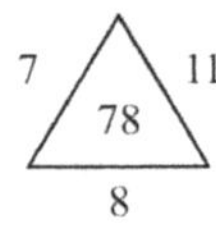 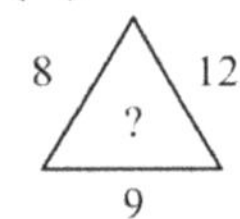

(A) 85   (B) 86
(C) 87   (D) 89

17. 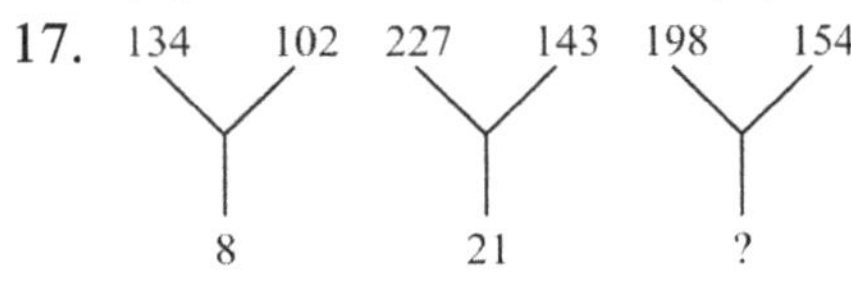

(A) 11   (B) 12
(C) 13   (D) 14

18. 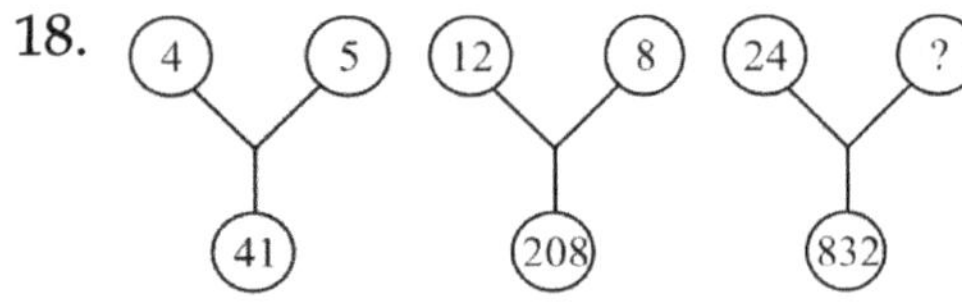

(A) 14   (B) 16
(C) 18   (D) 20

19. How many odd numbers are there in the sequence each of which is immediately followed by an odd number?

5 1 4 7 3 9 8 5 7 2 6 3 1 5 8 6 3 8 5 2 2 4 3 4 9 6

(A) 3   (B) 5
(C) 6   (D) 4

20. How many odd numbers are there in the sequence which are immediately preceded and also immediately followed by an even number in the sequence ?

5 1 4 7 3 2 5 6 8 9 6 7 3 2 1 5 6 4 3 2 7 4

(A) 4   (B) 3
(C) 5   (D) 2

21. How many even numbers are there which are immediately followed by an odd number and also immediately preceded by an odd number in the sequence?

8 4 7 6 5 3 2 5 1 6 4 3 2 6 7 9 8 5

(A) 3   (B) 4
(C) 2   (D) 15

Direction (1 to 11): In each of the following problems, find the number of triangles in the given figure :

22. 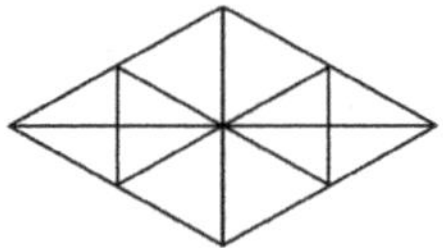

(A) 22   (B) 24
(C) 28   (D) 32

23. 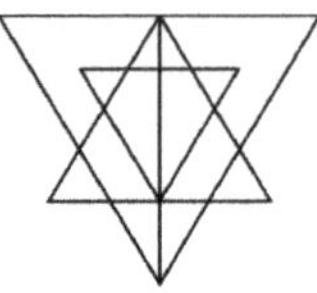

(A) 22   (B) 23
(C) 25   (D) 27

24. 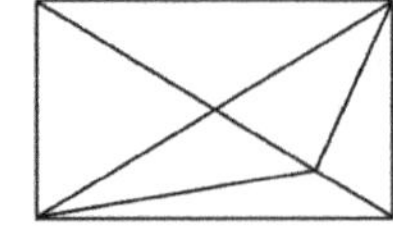

(A) 14   (B) 15
(C) 16   (D) 17

Direction (25 to 27): In the given figure, there are three intersecting circles, each representing certain section of people.

Different regions are marked p, d, r, s, t, u, v. Read the statement in the given question and choose the letter of the region which correctly represents the statement.

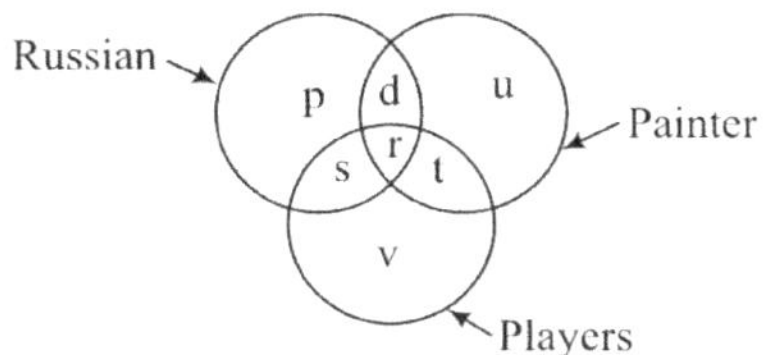

25. Russian who are painters but not players.

(A) d   (B) t
(C) s   (D) v

26. Russian who are painters as well as players.

(A) p   (B) d
(C) r   (D) s

27. Russian who are players but not painters.

(A) p   (B) d
(C) r   (D) s

Direction: In each of the following questions, fig. (X) is embedded in one of the four alterative figures (A), (B), (C) or (D). Find the alternative which contains fig. (X) as its part.

28.
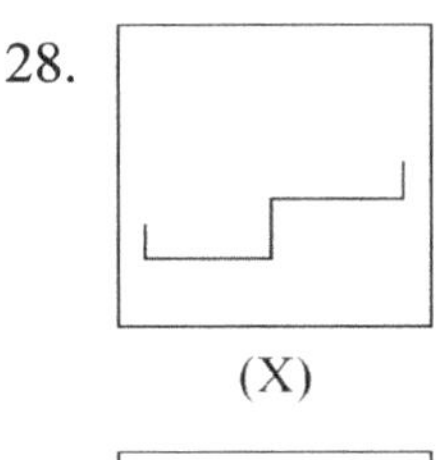
(X)
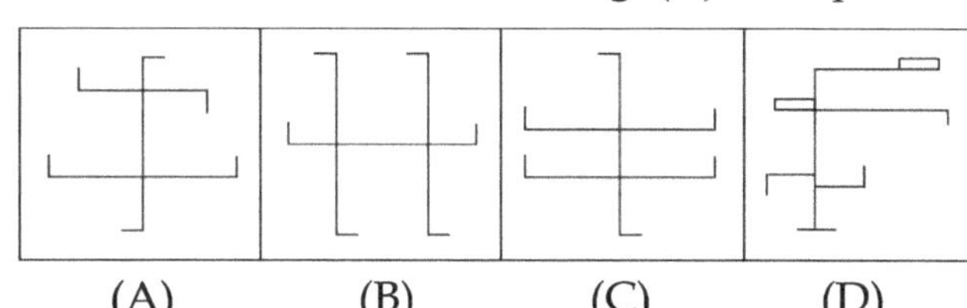
(A)   (B)   (C)   (D)

29.
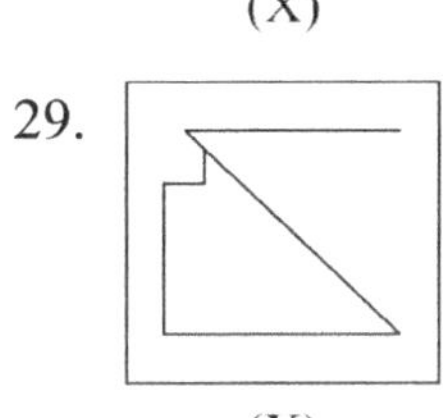
(X)
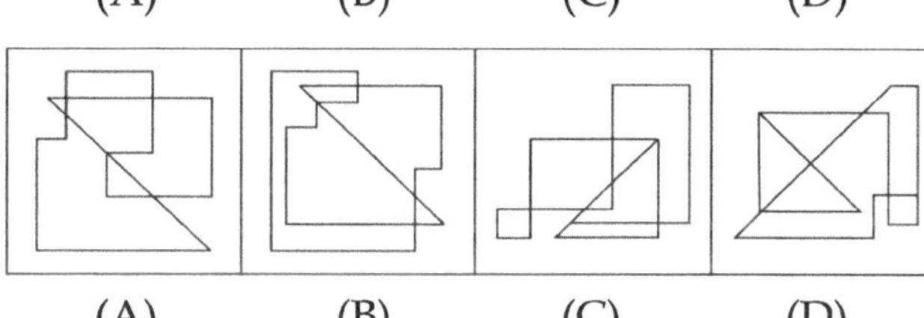
(A)   (B)   (C)   (D)

30.
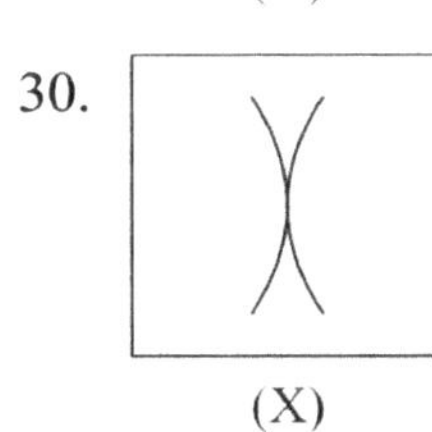
(X)
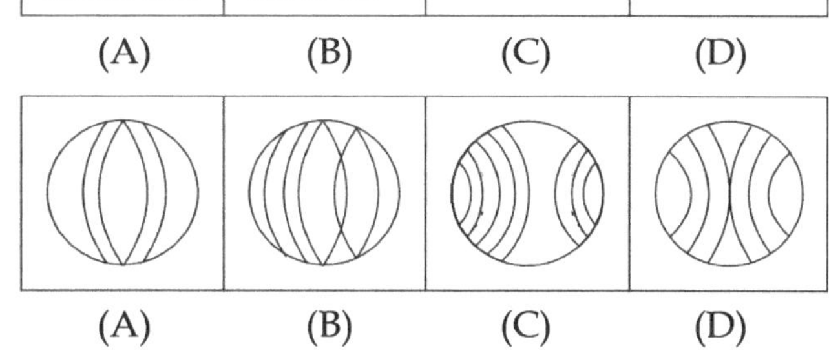
(A)   (B)   (C)   (D)

Direction (31-33): In the following problems, select a figure from amongst the four options which when placed in the blank space of figure (X) would complete the pattern.

31.
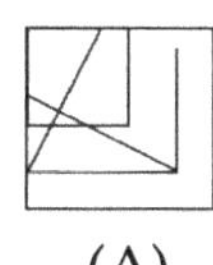
(X)
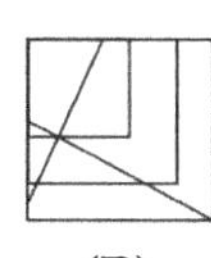
(A)
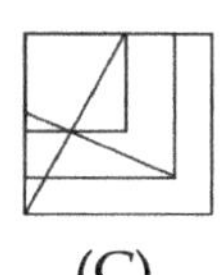
(B)
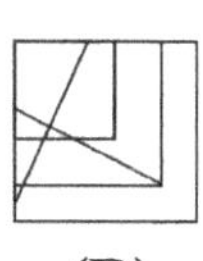
(C)   (D)

32. 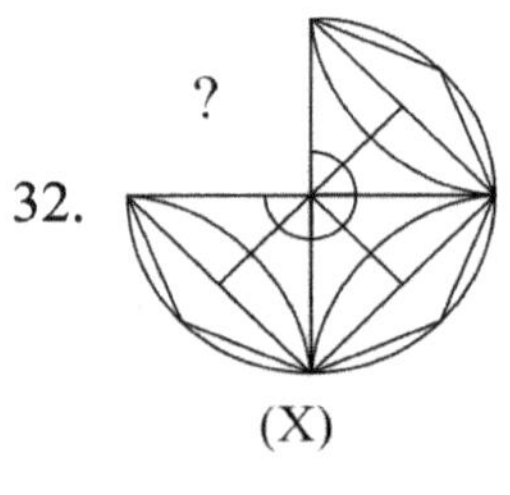
(X)   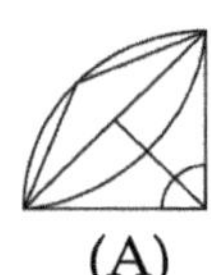 (A)   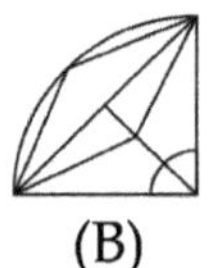 (B)   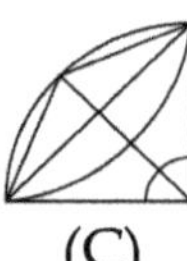 (C)    (D)

33. 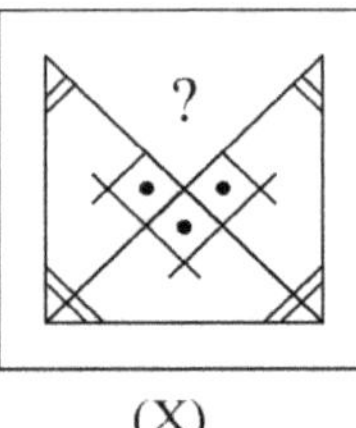
(X)   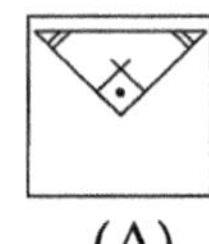 (A)   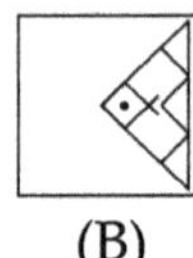 (B)   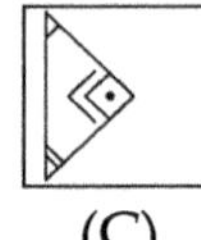 (C)   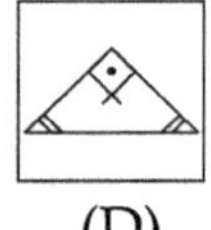 (D)

Direction (34 to 36): In each of the following questions, you are given a combination of alphabets and/or numbers followed by four alternatives (A), (B), (C) and (D). Choose the alternative which most closely resembles the water-image of the given combination.

34. DISC
(A) CSID
(B) ƆSIⱭ
(C) DIꙄC
(D) DISC

35. FROG
(A) ⅎꓤOƆ
(B) GORF
(C) ꓒOꓤⅎ
(D) ⅎꓤOG

36. RECRUIT
(A) ꓤECꓤUIꓕ
(B) ꓤECꓤUIꓕ
(C) RECRUIT
(D) ꓕIUꓤCEꓤ

37. 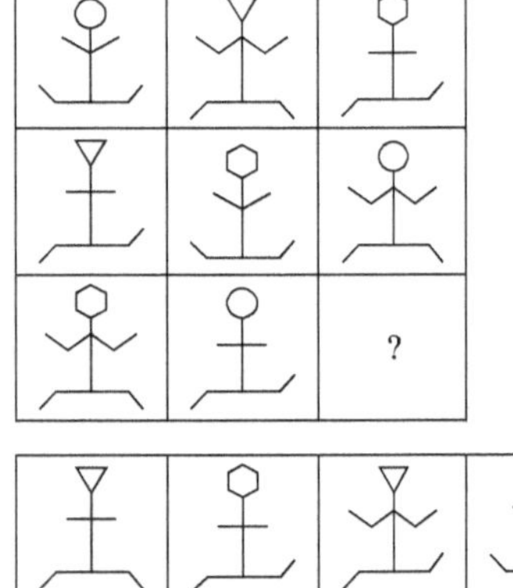
(A)   (B)   (C)   (D)

38. 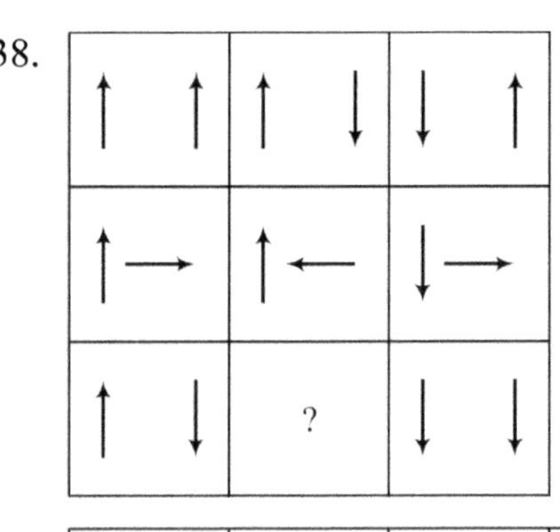
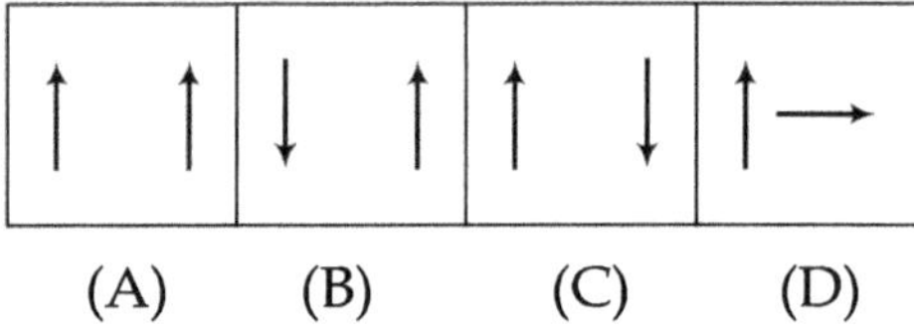
(A)   (B)   (C)   (D)

39.

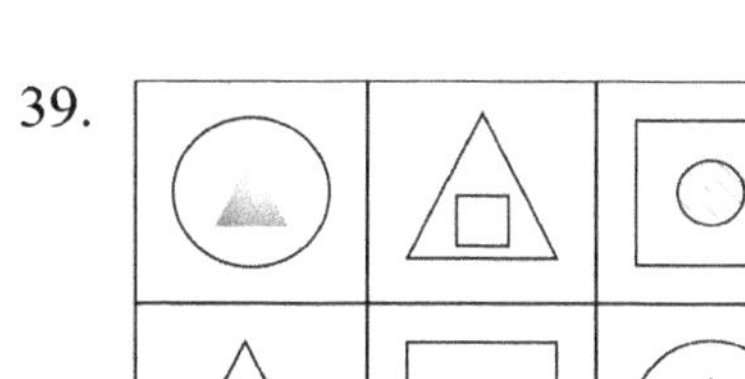

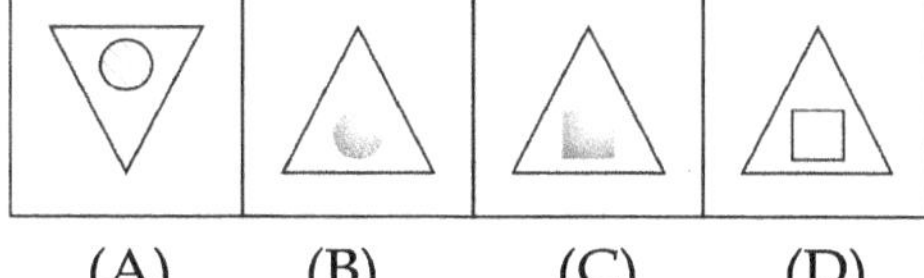

(A)	(B)	(C)	(D)

40.

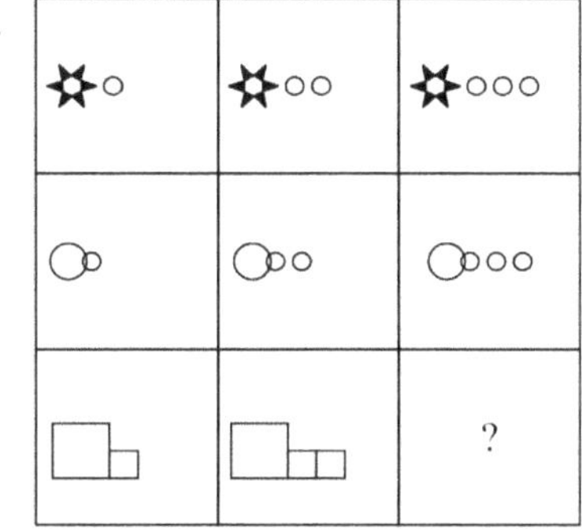

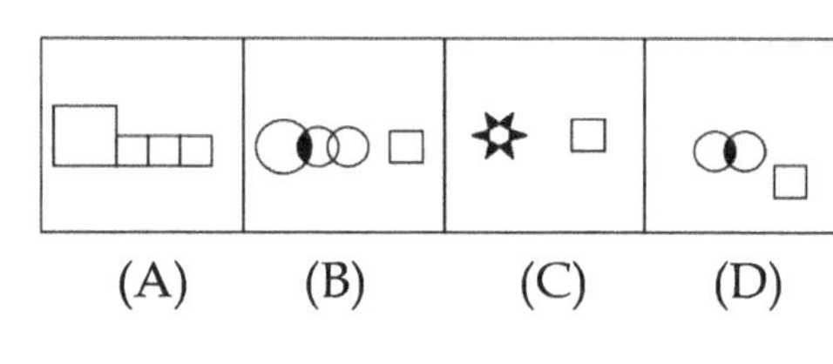

(A)	(B)	(C)	(D)

1.	Ⓐ Ⓑ Ⓒ Ⓓ	9.	Ⓐ Ⓑ Ⓒ Ⓓ	17.	Ⓐ Ⓑ Ⓒ Ⓓ	25.	Ⓐ Ⓑ Ⓒ Ⓓ	33.	Ⓐ Ⓑ Ⓒ Ⓓ
2.	Ⓐ Ⓑ Ⓒ Ⓓ	10.	Ⓐ Ⓑ Ⓒ Ⓓ	18.	Ⓐ Ⓑ Ⓒ Ⓓ	26.	Ⓐ Ⓑ Ⓒ Ⓓ	34.	Ⓐ Ⓑ Ⓒ Ⓓ
3.	Ⓐ Ⓑ Ⓒ Ⓓ	11.	Ⓐ Ⓑ Ⓒ Ⓓ	19.	Ⓐ Ⓑ Ⓒ Ⓓ	27.	Ⓐ Ⓑ Ⓒ Ⓓ	35.	Ⓐ Ⓑ Ⓒ Ⓓ
4.	Ⓐ Ⓑ Ⓒ Ⓓ	12.	Ⓐ Ⓑ Ⓒ Ⓓ	20.	Ⓐ Ⓑ Ⓒ Ⓓ	28.	Ⓐ Ⓑ Ⓒ Ⓓ	36.	Ⓐ Ⓑ Ⓒ Ⓓ
5.	Ⓐ Ⓑ Ⓒ Ⓓ	13.	Ⓐ Ⓑ Ⓒ Ⓓ	21.	Ⓐ Ⓑ Ⓒ Ⓓ	29.	Ⓐ Ⓑ Ⓒ Ⓓ	37.	Ⓐ Ⓑ Ⓒ Ⓓ
6.	Ⓐ Ⓑ Ⓒ Ⓓ	14.	Ⓐ Ⓑ Ⓒ Ⓓ	22.	Ⓐ Ⓑ Ⓒ Ⓓ	30.	Ⓐ Ⓑ Ⓒ Ⓓ	38.	Ⓐ Ⓑ Ⓒ Ⓓ
7.	Ⓐ Ⓑ Ⓒ Ⓓ	15.	Ⓐ Ⓑ Ⓒ Ⓓ	23.	Ⓐ Ⓑ Ⓒ Ⓓ	31.	Ⓐ Ⓑ Ⓒ Ⓓ	39.	Ⓐ Ⓑ Ⓒ Ⓓ
8.	Ⓐ Ⓑ Ⓒ Ⓓ	16.	Ⓐ Ⓑ Ⓒ Ⓓ	24.	Ⓐ Ⓑ Ⓒ Ⓓ	32.	Ⓐ Ⓑ Ⓒ Ⓓ	40.	Ⓐ Ⓑ Ⓒ Ⓓ

MODEL TEST PAPER

MULTIPLE CHOICE QUESTIONS

Section I: Logical Reasoning

1. If in a certain code, 'when' means 'x', 'you' means '÷','come' means '−' and 'will' means '+', then what will be the value of "8 when 12 will 16 you 2 come 10" ?
   (A) 45   (B) 94
   (C) 96   (D) 112

2. How many numbers from 11 to 50 are there, which are exactly divisible by 7 but not by 3?
   (A) Two   (B) Four
   (C) Five   (D) Six

3. The given table shows the ticket prices of an amusement park. Mohit sells tickets to 7 adults, 15 youth and 10 children. How much does he earn?

   Ticket Prices

Type of Tickets	Price
Child	₹ 20
Youth	₹ 15
Adult	₹ 20

   (A) ₹ 565   (B) ₹ 470
   (C) ₹ 500   (D) ₹ 865

4. Rahul bought 4 packets of notebook papers for school last year. Each packet contained 50 notebook papers. He used about 20 notebook papers every week. Find the number of notebook papers Rahul was left with after 7 weeks?
   (A) 67   (B) 17
   (C) 70   (D) 60

5. Priyanka is shorter than Shikha and longer than Sneha. If Sneha is longer than Yukti, who is the shortest among them?
   (A) Priyanka   (B) Shikha
   (C) Sneha   (D) Yukti

6. If 'paper' is called 'wood', 'wood' is called 'straw', 'straw' is called 'grass', 'grass' is called 'rubber' and 'rubber' is called 'cloth', what is furniture made up of ?
   (A) Paper   (B) Wood
   (C) Straw   (D) Grass

7. Ranbir is sixth from the left end and Vikram is tenth from the right end in a row of boys. If there are eight boys between Ranbir and Vikram, how many boys are there in that row?
   (A) 23   (B) 25
   (C) 24   (D) 26

8. How many squares are there in the given figure?

   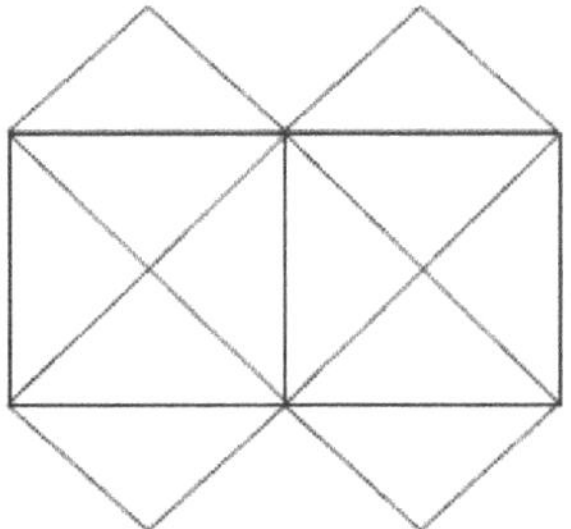

   (A) 6   (B) 7
   (C) 8   (D) 9

9. Which pair of eagle pictures shows reflection?
   (A)    (B) 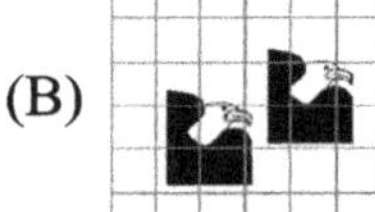

(C) 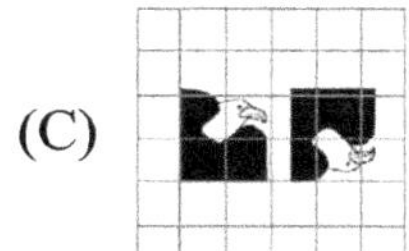   (D) 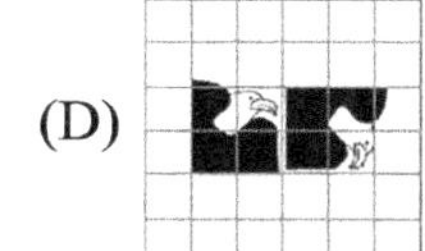

10. A parent group is planning an awards dinner for students, teachers and parents. The parent group plans to seat the guests around a circular table that has seating for 30. The guests will be seated in the order of student, teacher and parent in a repeating pattern. Who will be the 23rd guest?

   (A) Student

   (B) Teacher

   (C) Parent

   (D) Cannot be determined

11. A community swimming pool is open on different days depending on the air temperature. The given table shows the air temperature on different days. The dates listed in the table show that the pool was closed on July 1, August 1 and October 1. If the pool was open on all the other dates listed, which of the following statements best describes the air temperature when the pool is open?

Swimming Pool

Date	Air Temperature
May 1	68° F
June 1	73° F
July 1	82° F
August 1	87° F
September 1	80° F
October 1	95° F

   (A) The air temperature must be between 74° F and 90° F

   (B) The air temperature must be lower than 91° F

   (C) The air temperature must be higher than 75° F

   (D) The air temperature must be between 67° F and 81° F

12. Choose the correct mirror image of Figure (X), when the mirror is placed along PQ.

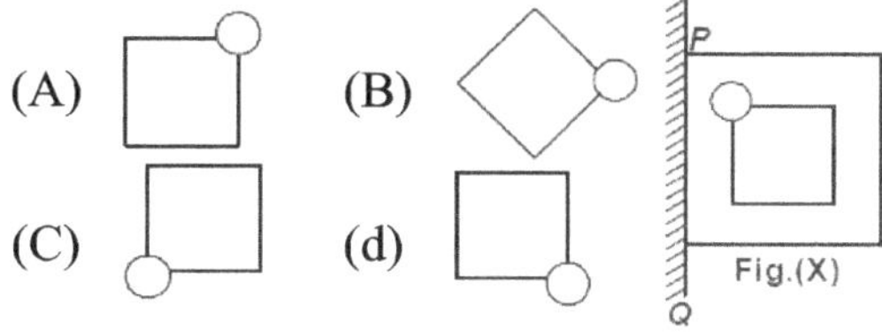

13. Which one of the following diagrams best illustrates the three classes : "Sailor, Ship, Ocean" ?

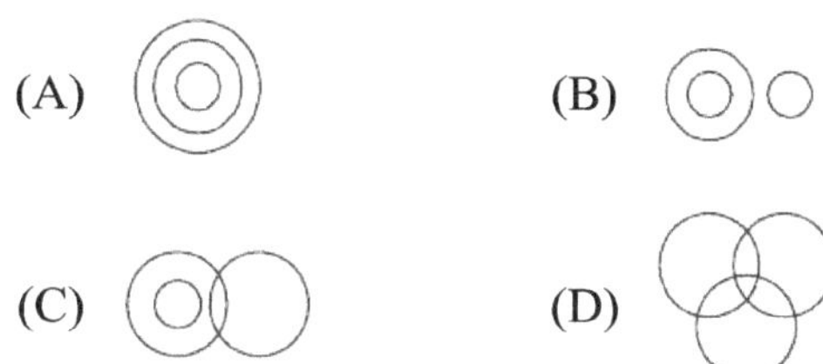

14. If 1st and 26th, 2nd and 25th, 3rd and 24th, and so on, the letters of the English alphabet are paired, which of the following pairs is correct?

   (A) GR

   (B) CW

   (C) IP

   (D) EV

15. Rohan plans to make a display by stacking cans. The top 3 rows are shown here. The display will be a total of 9 rows. How many cans in all will Rohan need to make the display?

   (A) 49

   (B) 45

   (C) 47

   (D) 42

16. A zoo had 17 tigers. All but eight died. How many were left with the zoo?

(A) Nil   (B) 8

(C) 9   (D) 17

17. Read the graph and answer the given question. On which day did Samir receive exactly 45 text messages?

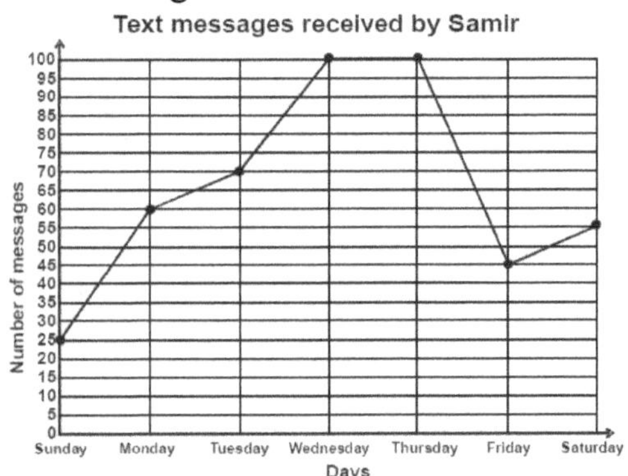

(A) Monday   (B) Thursday

(C) Friday   (D) Sunday

18. Armaan walks 30 metres towards south. Then, turning to right, he walks 30 metres. Then, turning to his left, he walks 20 metres. Again, he turns to his left and walks 30 metres. How far is he from his initial position?

(A) 20 metres   (B) 50 metres

(C) 60 metres   (D) 80 metres

19. How many lines of symmetry does the figure have?

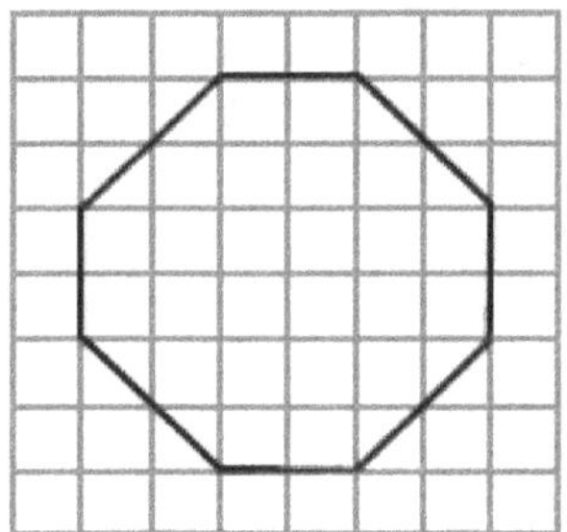

(A) 1   (B) 2

(C) 3   (D) 4

20. Find the odd one out.

(A) $176 - 168$ (B) $214 - 206$

(C) $577 - 568$ (D) $319 - 311$

Section II: Mathematical Reasoning

21. A mistake was made in simplifying the expression given below.

Simplify: $5 + 2(6 + 4)^2 - 2^3$,

Step 1: $5 + 2(10) - 2^3$,

Step 2: $5 + 20 - 8$,

Step 3: $25 - 8$,

Step 4: 17.

In which step did the first mistake appear?

(A) Step 1   (B) Step 2

(C) Step 3   (D) Step 4

22. What percentage of the figures are circles?

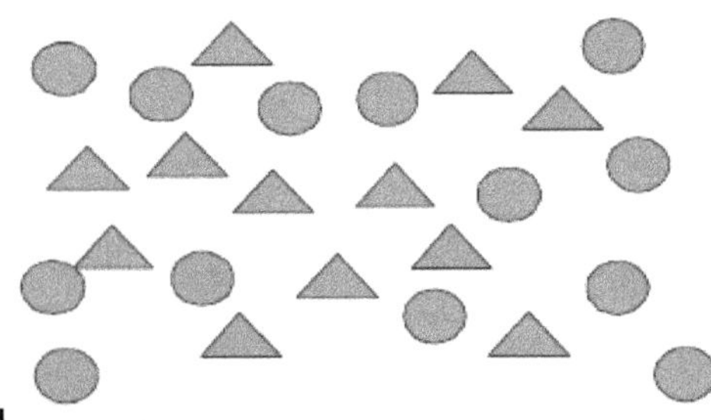

(A) 48%   (B) 50%

(C) 52%   (D) 54%

23. Find the value of the expression given below?

$$\left(\frac{3a^2 + 2a \times 5 - 4}{4} \right) + 5a - 2, \text{ when } a = 4$$

(A) 24   (B) 39

(C) 27   (D) 36

24. Which of the following figures has 10 vertices?

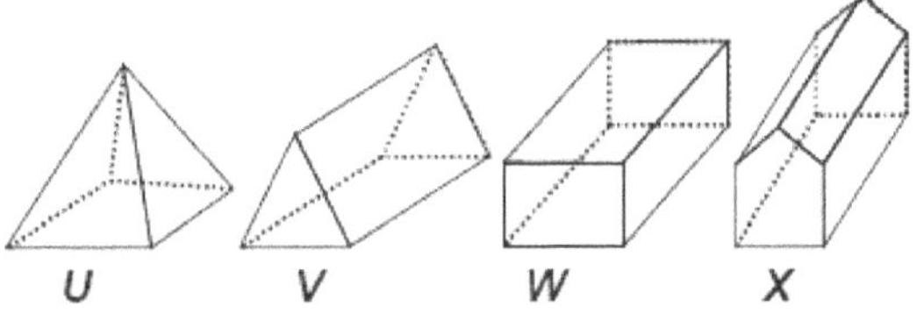

(A) Figure U   (B) Figure V

(C) Figure W   (D) Figure X

25. Which list of integers is in order from greatest to least ?
    (A) - 42, –39, – 4, 40, 41
    (B) - 42, 41, 40, – 39, – 4
    (C) - 4, – 39, 40, 41, 42
    (D) 41, 40, – 4, – 39, – 42

26. Which model best represents the expression $\dfrac{1}{2} \times \dfrac{1}{3}$?

(A) 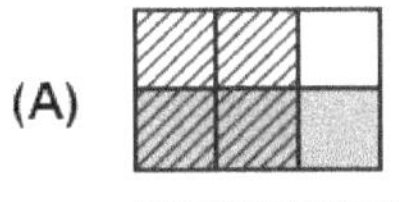

(B) 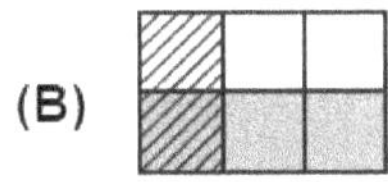

(C) 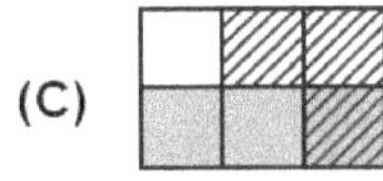

(D) 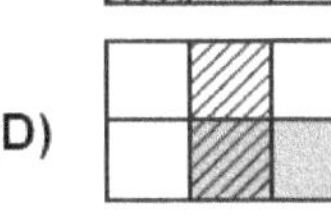

27. Mr. Sameer was trying to find a tablecloth for his rectangular dining table. He knew the area and perimeter of the tabletop.

    Area = 40 square metres, Perimeter = 28 metres

    Which of the following best represents the width and length of the tabletop?
    (A) Length = 10 m, Width = 4 m
    (B) Width = 2 m, Length = 20 m
    (C) Width = 5 m, Length = 8 m
    (D) Width = 4 m, Length = 12 m

28. If 2 unit cubes, one on each are placed on the unit cubes marked 'X', which solid will be obtained?

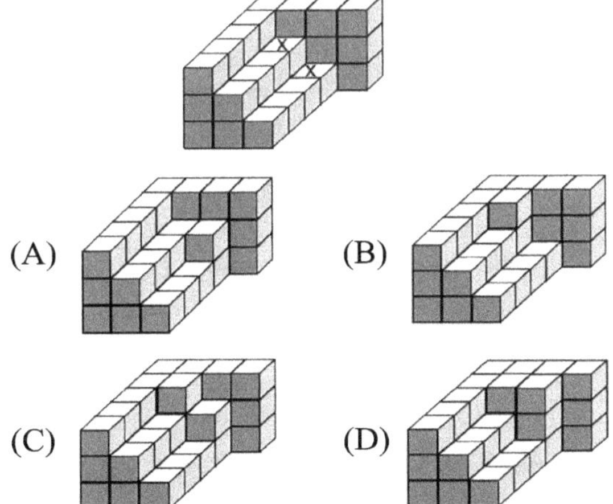

    (A)   (B)

    (C)   (D)

29. Fill in the blank of the statement given below.
    70 has ______ factors.
    (A) 2   (B) 4
    (C) 6   (D) 8

30. Which of the following is true for the two given congruent figures?

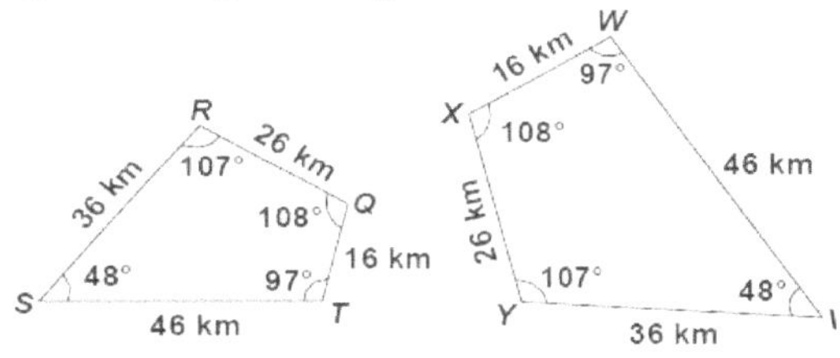

    (A) $\overline{TQ} \cong \overline{XY}$
    (B) $\overline{ST} \cong \overline{XY}$
    (C) $\overline{TQ} \cong \overline{WX}$
    (D) $\angle Q \cong \angle Y$

31. The total cost of 5 teddy bears is the same as the total cost of 9 clowns. Find the cost of a teddy bear.

    (A) Rs. 27   (B) Rs. 28
    (C) Rs. 30   (D) Rs. 32

32. The perimeter of the given figure is _____.

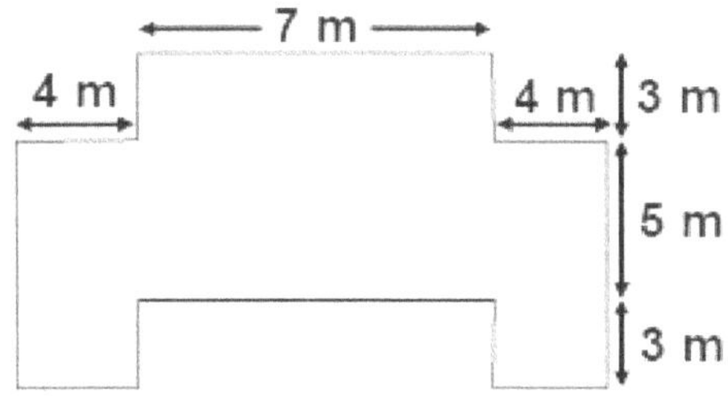

    (A) 68 m
    (B) 48 m
    (C) 58 m
    (D) 50 m

33. Which of the following digits makes the given statement true?

The number 606__19 is divisible by 9.

(A) 3   (B) 6   (C) 5   (D) 8

34. Given that,

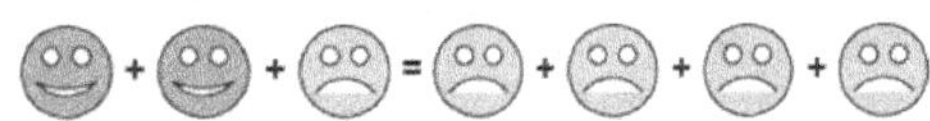

If each 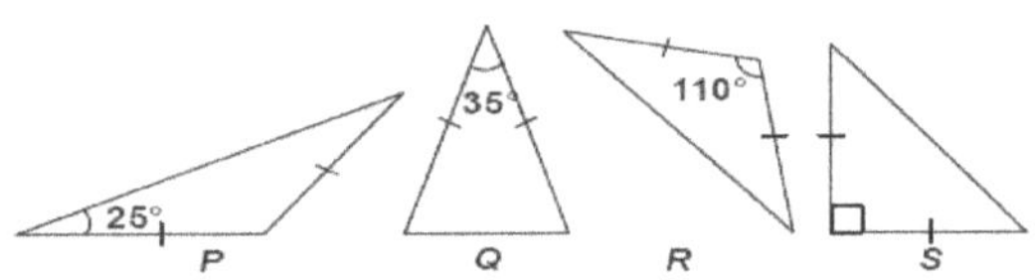 stands for $\frac{1}{4}$, what does each stand for ?

(A) 3/4   (B) 3/2

(C) 3/8   (D) 3/5

35. Asha looked at different flower arrangements before purchasing one. The arrangements varied in price from Rs.15.62 to Rs. 37.50. Which measure of data can be used to describe the variation between maximum and minimum price?

(A) Mean   (B) Mode

(C) Range   (D) Median

36. Which of the following figures are acute isosceles triangles ?

(A) P only   (B) Q only

(C) R only   (D) R and S only

37. Evaluate:

$$\frac{3}{4} + 5\frac{1}{2} - 1\frac{1}{3} - \frac{1}{2} \times \frac{9}{10}$$

(A) 4.48   (B) −4.46

(C) −4.82   (D) 4.46

38. Ashwin used the rule listed below to rewrite the expression $10^2 \times 10^5 = 10^7$.

$$10^m \times 10^n = 10^{m+n}$$

Based on this rule, which of the following is equivalent to the expression $8^{-8} \times 8^6$?

(A) 8^{-10}, because $8^{-4} \times 8^6 = 8^{-4+6}$

(B) 8^{-12}, because $8^{-4} \times 8^{-8} = 8^{-4-8}$

(C) 8^{-2}, because $8^{-8} \times 8^6 = 8^{-8+6}$

(D) 8^2, because $8^{-4} \times 8^6 = 8^{-4+6}$

39. A building is 24 m long. The bottom of the ladder is 10 m away from the foot of the building. Find the length of the ladder?

(A) 12 m   (B) 24 m

(C) 26 m   (D) 8 m

40. Amit counted the number of people in line for tickets at the movie theatre. Every time he saw 7 people, he added a tick mark on his counting sheet, as shown below.

✓✓✓✓✓✓✓✓✓✓✓✓✓✓✓✓

Amit saw 6 more people after he added his last tick mark. Which expression can be used to find u, the total number of people he saw?

(A) $16 \div 6 + 7 = u$ (B) $16 \times 6 \times 7 = u$

(C) $16 \times 7 + 6 = u$ (D) $16 + 7 - 6 = u$

Section III: Everyday Mathematics

41. It took Abhilasha 20 minutes to apply a coat of paint to a piece of pottery. After each coat she waited for 1 hour 30 minutes for the paint to dry. Which is a reasonable amount of time it could have taken for Abhilasha to have applied 5 coats of paint and for the pottery to be completely dry ?

(A) 505 minutes   (B) 8 hours

(C) 195 minutes   (D) 9 hours

42. The average of three numbers is $9m + 8$. Two of the three numbers are $2m + 3$ and $4m + 5$. Express the third number in terms of m in the simplest form.

(A) $9m + 8$ (B) $27m + 24$

(C) $21m + 16$ (D) $21m + 32$

43. Hrishant packs boxes for an appliance company. He can pack a large box in 10 minutes and a small box in 4 minutes. He needs to pack 10 large boxes and 20 small boxes. If he starts his work 3.5 hours before closing time, will Hrishant have time to finish the work before closing time if he works without stopping?

(A) Yes, Hrishant will finish the work in 3 hours.

(B) No, it will take Hrishant 4 hours to finish.

(C) Yes, Hrishant will finish the work in 2.5 hours.

(D) No, it will take Hrishant 6 hours to finish.

44. The total length of all songs on a CD, Anshuman bought is about 74 minutes. Each song is between 4 to 6 minutes long. Which is a reasonable number of songs that could be on the CD?

(A) 10   (B) 40

(C) 74   (D) 16

45. Ishika and Sasha raced their toy cars. The given diagram shows the distance travelled by the cars during the race. How far did Ishika's car travel than Sasha's car?

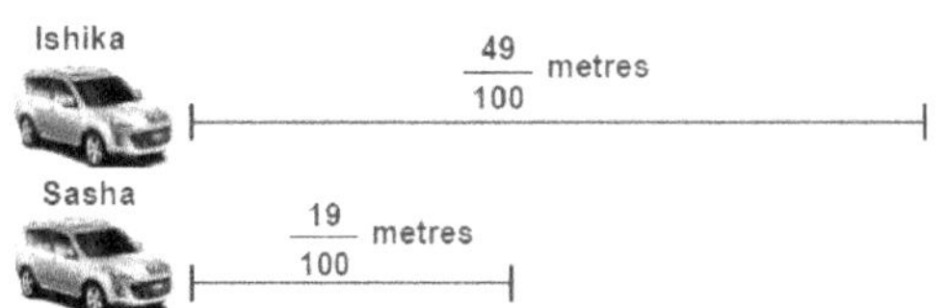

(A) 3/10 m   (B) 4/10 m

(C) 32/10 m   (D) 68 /100 m

46. Tameena has 4 old coins : P, Q, R and S. Coin R is worth Rs. 2.5. Coin S is worth 2 times the value of coin R. Coin Q is worth 3 times the value of coin R. The four coins are worth Rs. 40 altogether. What is the value of coin P?

(A) Rs. 14   (B) Rs. 18

(C) Rs. 25   (D) Rs. 15

47. Ankit can run 100 metres in 12.5 seconds. If he competes in the 400 metres race, about how many seconds will he take to run the race?

(A) 50 seconds   (B) 40 seconds

(C) 80 seconds   (D) 20 seconds

48. Misha answered 56% of the 150 problems on her history homework correctly. How many problems on her homework did she answer correctly?

(A) 56   (B) 65

(C) 84   (D) 92

49. There are 338 cows and goats on a farm. $\frac{2}{3}$ of the cows are equal to $\frac{1}{5}$ of the goats on the farm. How many cows are there on the farm?

(A) 78   (B) 260

(C) 72   (D) 270

50. Which of the following statements represents the greatest percent of change?

(A) A tree grew from 6 feet to 12 feet in 1 year.

(B) An aquarium that was originally priced at Rs. 90 is now priced at Rs.140.

(C) A person whose salary was Rs. 1000 per week is now earning Rs. 1500 per week.

(D) A baby who weighed 5 pounds at birth now weighs 20 pounds.

—Darken Your Choice with HB Pencil—

1.	Ⓐ Ⓑ Ⓒ Ⓓ	11.	Ⓐ Ⓑ Ⓒ Ⓓ	21.	Ⓐ Ⓑ Ⓒ Ⓓ	31.	Ⓐ Ⓑ Ⓒ Ⓓ	41.	Ⓐ Ⓑ Ⓒ Ⓓ
2.	Ⓐ Ⓑ Ⓒ Ⓓ	12.	Ⓐ Ⓑ Ⓒ Ⓓ	22.	Ⓐ Ⓑ Ⓒ Ⓓ	32.	Ⓐ Ⓑ Ⓒ Ⓓ	42.	Ⓐ Ⓑ Ⓒ Ⓓ
3.	Ⓐ Ⓑ Ⓒ Ⓓ	13.	Ⓐ Ⓑ Ⓒ Ⓓ	23.	Ⓐ Ⓑ Ⓒ Ⓓ	33.	Ⓐ Ⓑ Ⓒ Ⓓ	43.	Ⓐ Ⓑ Ⓒ Ⓓ
4.	Ⓐ Ⓑ Ⓒ Ⓓ	14.	Ⓐ Ⓑ Ⓒ Ⓓ	24.	Ⓐ Ⓑ Ⓒ Ⓓ	34.	Ⓐ Ⓑ Ⓒ Ⓓ	44.	Ⓐ Ⓑ Ⓒ Ⓓ
5.	Ⓐ Ⓑ Ⓒ Ⓓ	15.	Ⓐ Ⓑ Ⓒ Ⓓ	25.	Ⓐ Ⓑ Ⓒ Ⓓ	35.	Ⓐ Ⓑ Ⓒ Ⓓ	45.	Ⓐ Ⓑ Ⓒ Ⓓ
6.	Ⓐ Ⓑ Ⓒ Ⓓ	16.	Ⓐ Ⓑ Ⓒ Ⓓ	26.	Ⓐ Ⓑ Ⓒ Ⓓ	36.	Ⓐ Ⓑ Ⓒ Ⓓ	46.	Ⓐ Ⓑ Ⓒ Ⓓ
7.	Ⓐ Ⓑ Ⓒ Ⓓ	17.	Ⓐ Ⓑ Ⓒ Ⓓ	27.	Ⓐ Ⓑ Ⓒ Ⓓ	37.	Ⓐ Ⓑ Ⓒ Ⓓ	47.	Ⓐ Ⓑ Ⓒ Ⓓ
8.	Ⓐ Ⓑ Ⓒ Ⓓ	18.	Ⓐ Ⓑ Ⓒ Ⓓ	28.	Ⓐ Ⓑ Ⓒ Ⓓ	38.	Ⓐ Ⓑ Ⓒ Ⓓ	48.	Ⓐ Ⓑ Ⓒ Ⓓ
9.	Ⓐ Ⓑ Ⓒ Ⓓ	19.	Ⓐ Ⓑ Ⓒ Ⓓ	29.	Ⓐ Ⓑ Ⓒ Ⓓ	39.	Ⓐ Ⓑ Ⓒ Ⓓ	49.	Ⓐ Ⓑ Ⓒ Ⓓ
10.	Ⓐ Ⓑ Ⓒ Ⓓ	20.	Ⓐ Ⓑ Ⓒ Ⓓ	30.	Ⓐ Ⓑ Ⓒ Ⓓ	40.	Ⓐ Ⓑ Ⓒ Ⓓ	50.	Ⓐ Ⓑ Ⓒ Ⓓ

HINTS AND SOLUTIONS

1. RATIONAL NUMBERS

Answer Key

1. (B)	2. (A)	3. (A)	4. (A)	5. (B)	6. (C)	7. (B)	8. (D)	9. (B)	10. (A)
11. (C)	12. (C)	13. (B)	14. (A)	15. (B)	16. (D)	17. (A)	18. (A)	19. (D)	20. (D)

1. (B)

Let the number be x.

$$\therefore \quad \frac{-15}{14} \times x = \frac{-16}{35}$$

$$\Rightarrow \quad x = \frac{-16}{35} \times \frac{14}{-15} = \frac{32}{75}$$

2. (A)

Let x be the number that should be subtracted

$$\therefore \frac{-5}{3} - x = \frac{5}{6}$$

$$\Rightarrow \quad x = \frac{-5}{3} - \frac{5}{6} = \frac{-10-5}{6}$$

$$\Rightarrow \quad x = \frac{-15}{6} = \frac{-5}{2}$$

3. (A)

If x is the additive inverse then $\dfrac{-7}{9} + x = 0$

$$\Rightarrow \quad x = \frac{7}{9}$$

4. (A)

$$x + \left(\frac{-10}{3}\right) = -3$$

$$\Rightarrow \quad x = \frac{10}{3} - 3 = \frac{10-9}{3} = \frac{1}{3}$$

5. (B)

Cost of one metre of cloth $= \dfrac{78\frac{3}{4}}{7\frac{1}{2}} = \dfrac{\frac{315}{4}}{\frac{15}{2}}$

$$= \frac{315}{4} \times \frac{2}{15} = \frac{21}{2} = ₹10\frac{1}{2}$$

6. (C)

$$\frac{-33}{8} \div x = \frac{-11}{2}$$

$$\Rightarrow \quad \frac{-33}{8} \times \frac{1}{x} = \frac{-11}{2} \Rightarrow x = \frac{-33}{8} \times \frac{2}{-11}$$

$$\Rightarrow \quad x = \frac{3}{4}$$

7. (B)

$$\frac{-16}{63} \times x = \frac{-4}{7}$$

$$x = \frac{-4}{7} \times \frac{63}{-16} = \frac{9}{4}$$

8. (D)

$$\frac{-7}{8} + x = \frac{4}{9} \qquad \Rightarrow x = \frac{4}{9} + \frac{7}{8} = \frac{32+63}{72}$$

$$\Rightarrow \quad x = \frac{95}{72}$$

9. (B)

We have $\dfrac{1}{2} + \dfrac{1}{5} = \dfrac{5+2}{10} = \dfrac{7}{10}$

$\therefore$ Reciprocal of $\left(\dfrac{1}{2} + \dfrac{1}{5}\right) = \dfrac{10}{7}$

10. (A)

$$\dfrac{\left(\dfrac{-2}{3} + \dfrac{1}{4}\right)}{2} = \dfrac{\dfrac{-8+3}{12}}{2} = \dfrac{-5}{24}$$

11. (C)

$$\dfrac{1}{5} \times \dfrac{2}{5} \div \dfrac{4}{5} = \dfrac{1}{5} \times \dfrac{2}{5} \times \dfrac{5}{4} = \dfrac{1}{10}$$

$\therefore$ Reciprocal $= \dfrac{1}{\dfrac{1}{10}} = 10.$

12. (C)

Let x be added.

$\therefore \dfrac{-3}{5} + x = \dfrac{-1}{3} \Rightarrow x = \dfrac{3}{5} - \dfrac{1}{3} = \dfrac{9-5}{15} = \dfrac{4}{15}$

13. (B)

$$\dfrac{3}{4} - \dfrac{2}{3} + \dfrac{1}{5} = \dfrac{45 - 40 + 12}{60} = \dfrac{17}{60}$$

Additive inverse of $\dfrac{17}{60}$ is $\dfrac{-17}{60}$.

14. (A)

$$\dfrac{3}{4} \div \dfrac{5}{8} \times \dfrac{3}{7} + \dfrac{2}{9} - \dfrac{1}{3}$$

$$= \dfrac{3}{4} \times \dfrac{8}{5} \times \dfrac{3}{7} + \dfrac{2}{9} - \dfrac{1}{3} = \dfrac{18}{35} + \dfrac{2}{9} - \dfrac{1}{3}$$

$$= \dfrac{162 + 70 - 105}{315} = \dfrac{232 - 105}{315} = \dfrac{127}{315}$$

15. (B)

Here $2 - \left[5 - \left\{4 - \dfrac{3}{2}\left(2 - \dfrac{2}{3}\right)\right\}\right]$

$$= 2 - \left[5 - \left\{4 - \dfrac{3}{2}\left(\dfrac{4}{3}\right)\right\}\right] = 2 - [5 - \{4 - 2\}]$$

$$= 2 - [5 - 2] = 2 - 3 = -1.$$

16. (D)

18. (A)

LCM of $9, 12, 18, 3 = 36$

$\therefore \dfrac{4}{-9} = \dfrac{16}{-36}; \dfrac{-5}{12} = \dfrac{15}{-36}; \dfrac{7}{-18} = \dfrac{14}{-36}$

$\dfrac{2}{-3} = \dfrac{24}{-36}$

19. (D)

LCM of $12, 6, 18, 24 = 72$

$\dfrac{-7}{12} = \dfrac{-42}{72}; \dfrac{-5}{6} = \dfrac{-60}{72}$

$\dfrac{13}{-18} = \dfrac{-52}{72}; \dfrac{-23}{24} = \dfrac{-69}{72}$

20. (D)

Closure property of rational numbers is satisfied for addition, subtraction and multiplication.

Closure property : The sum of two rational numbers will be a rational number.

HOTS (ACHIEVERS SECTION)

21. (A)	22. (A)	23. (C)	24. (D)	25. (A)

21. (A)

Total no. of outcomes $= 8 \times 8 = 64$

Both numbers are even,

$\{(2,2)\,(2,6)\,(2,8)\,(2,4)\,(4,2)\,(4,4),\,(4,6)$
$(4,8),\,(6,2),\,(6,4)\,(6,6),\,(6,8)\,(8,2)\,(8,4)$
$(8,6),\,(8,8)\}$.

Required probability $= \dfrac{16}{64} = \dfrac{1}{4}$

22. (A)

Total number of letters $= 9$

Number of letter 'O' $= 3$

Required probability $= \dfrac{3}{9} = \dfrac{1}{3}$

23. (C)

$\dfrac{4}{9} - \dfrac{8}{13} = \dfrac{52 - 72}{117} = \dfrac{-20}{117}$

$\dfrac{-20}{117} \times \dfrac{169}{2} = \dfrac{-10 \times 13}{9} = \dfrac{-130}{9}$

$\dfrac{-130}{9} + \dfrac{1}{3} = \dfrac{-127}{9}$

2. LINEAR EQUATIONS IN ONE VARIABLE

Answer Key

1. (A)	2. (B)	3. (A)	4. (B)	5. (C)	6. (C)	7. (A)	8. (A)	9. (A)	10. (D)
11. (B)	12. (A)	13. (A)	14. (D)	15. (C)	16. (C)	17. (A)	18. (A)	19. (A)	20. (D)

1. (A)

Let the speed of boat in still water be x km/hour.

$\therefore \qquad (x + 2)\,4 = (x - 2)\,5$

$\Rightarrow \qquad 4x + 8 = 5x - 10$

$\Rightarrow \qquad x = 18$ km/hr

2. (B)

Let Mohan's age $= 9x$

and Sohan's age $= 7x$

10, years ago,

Mohan's age $= 9x - 10$

Sohan's age $= 7x - 10$

$\therefore \qquad \dfrac{9x - 10}{7x - 10} = \dfrac{7}{5}$

$\Rightarrow \qquad 45x - 50 = 49x - 70$

$\Rightarrow \qquad 4x = 20 \Rightarrow x = 5$

$\therefore$ Mohan's age $= 9 \times 5 = 45$

and Sohan's age $= 7 \times 5 = 35$

Hence difference $= 45 - 35 = 10$ years

3. (A)

Let the one number be x.

Other number $= 360 - x$

Now 65% of $x = 85\%$ of $(360 - x)$

$\Rightarrow \qquad \dfrac{65 \times x}{100} = \dfrac{85(360 - x)}{100}$

$\Rightarrow \quad 65\,x + 85x = 85 \times 360$

$\Rightarrow \qquad 150x = 85 \times 360$

$\Rightarrow \qquad x = \dfrac{85 \times 360}{150} = 204$

Other number $= 360 - 204 = 156$.

$\therefore$ Largest number $= 204$.

4. (B)

Let the no. of workers in the begining be x.

$\therefore \qquad 70 \times x = (x - 20)\,80$

$\Rightarrow \qquad 70\,x = 80x - 20 \times 80$

$\Rightarrow \qquad 10x = 20 \times 80$

$\Rightarrow \qquad x = \dfrac{20 \times 80}{10} = 160$

5. (C)

Let the numbers be

$\qquad 11x,\ 11(x + 1),\ 11(x + 2)$

Hence $11x + 11(x + 1) + 11(x + 2) = 363$

$\Rightarrow 11x + 11x + 11 + 11x + 22 = 363$

$\Rightarrow \qquad 33x + 33 = 363$

$$\Rightarrow \qquad x = \frac{330}{33} = 10$$

Greatest multiple $= 11(x + 2)$
$= 11\,(10 + 2) = 11 \times 12 = 132$

6. (C)

Let Son's age $= x$ years
$\therefore$ Arun's age $= 3x$.
Now 10 years ago, son's age $= x - 10$.
Given Arun's age $= 3x - 10$
$$\Rightarrow \qquad 3x - 10 = 5\,(x - 10)$$
$$\Rightarrow \qquad 3x - 10 = 5x - 50$$
$$2x = 40 \Rightarrow x = 20 \text{ years}$$
Arun's age $= 3 \times 20 = 60$ years
Sum of Arun's and Son's age $= 20 + 60$
$$= 80 \text{ years}$$

7. (A)

Let the number be x.
$$8\left(x - \frac{5}{2} \right) = 3x$$
$$\Rightarrow \qquad 8x - 20 = 3x$$
$$\Rightarrow \qquad 5x = 20$$
$$\Rightarrow \qquad x = 4$$

8. (A)

Let the unit's digit be x.
Ten's digit $= x + 3$.
Original number $= 10(x + 3) + 1(x)$
$$= 10x + 30 + x$$
$$= 11x + 30$$
After interchange, resulting number
$$= 10\,(x) + 1\,(x + 3)$$
$$= 10x + x + 3$$
$$= 11x + 3$$
$\therefore \qquad 11x + 3 + 11x + 30 = 143$
$$\Rightarrow \qquad 22x + 33 = 143$$
$$\Rightarrow \qquad 22x = 143 - 33$$
$$\Rightarrow \qquad 22x = 110$$
$$\Rightarrow \qquad x = \frac{110}{22} = 5$$

Original number $= 11x + 3 = 11 \times 5 + 3$

$$= 55 + 3 = 58$$

9. (A)

Let the age of grand son be x years.
Grand father's age $= 10x$.
$$\Rightarrow \qquad 10x = 54 + x$$
$$\Rightarrow \qquad 9x = 54$$
$$\Rightarrow \qquad x = 6$$
Grand father's age $= 10 \times 6 = 60$ years
sum of their present ages $= 60 + 6 = 66$.

10. (D)

Let the base be x.
$$\text{Altitude} = \frac{5}{3}\,x$$
$$\text{Area} = \frac{1}{2} \times x \times \frac{5}{3}\,x$$
$$\Rightarrow \frac{1}{2} \times x \times \frac{5}{3}\,x = \frac{1}{2} \times \left(\frac{5x}{3} + 4 \right)(x - 2)$$
$$\Rightarrow \qquad \frac{5x^2}{3} = \frac{5x^2}{3} - \frac{10x}{3} + 4x - 8$$
$$\Rightarrow 12x - 10x = 24 \Rightarrow x = \frac{24}{2} = 12$$
$$\therefore \text{ Altitude} = 12 \times 5/3 = 20 \text{ cm}$$

11. (B)

Let the area of the field ploughed daily be x hectares.
Area of the field $= 18x$
$$\Rightarrow \qquad 18x = (x + 16)\,12$$
$$\Rightarrow \qquad 18x = 12x + 16 \times 12$$
$$\Rightarrow \qquad 6x = 16 \times 12$$
$$\Rightarrow \qquad x = \frac{16 \times 12}{6} = 32$$
Area of the field $= 18 \times 32 = 576$ hectares

12. (A)

Let the unit's digit be x.
Ten's digit $= 9 - x$
Number $= 10\,(9 - x) + 1(x)$
$$= 90 - 10x + x = 90 - 9x$$
$$90 - 9x - 9 = x(10) + 1(9 - x)$$
$$\Rightarrow \qquad 81 - 9x = 10x + 9 - x$$

$\Rightarrow \quad 81 - 9x = 9x + 9$

$\Rightarrow \quad 18x = 72 \Rightarrow x = 4$

Number $= 90 - 9 \times 4 = 90 - 36 = 54$

13. (A)

Here $\dfrac{5(x+6) - 15(2-x)}{3x - 1} = 10$

$\Rightarrow 5x + 30 - 30 + 15x = 30x - 10$

$\Rightarrow \quad 20x + 10 = 30x$

$\Rightarrow \quad 10x = 10 \Rightarrow x = 1$

14. (D)

Here $\dfrac{3x+1}{16} + \dfrac{2x-3}{7} = \dfrac{x+3}{8} + \dfrac{3x-1}{14}$

$\Rightarrow \dfrac{21x + 7 + 32x - 48}{112} = \dfrac{14x + 42 + 24x - 8}{112}$

$\Rightarrow \quad 53x - 41 = 38x + 34$

$\Rightarrow \quad 15x = 34 + 41$

$\Rightarrow \quad x = \dfrac{75}{15} = 5$

15. (C)

Given $\quad \dfrac{x-n}{m+n} = \dfrac{x+n}{m-n}$

$\Rightarrow \quad (x-n)(m-n) = (x+n)(m+n)$

$\Rightarrow mx - mn - nx + n^2 = mx + mn + nx + n^2$

$\Rightarrow \quad -mn - nx = mn + nx$

$\Rightarrow \quad 2nx = -2mn$

$\Rightarrow \quad x = \dfrac{-2mn}{2n} = -m$

16. (C)

Let the cost price of the shirt be ₹ x.

$\therefore \quad x + 7\% \text{ of } x = 1498$

$\Rightarrow \quad x + \dfrac{7x}{100} = 1498$

$\Rightarrow \quad 107\, x = 1498 \times 100$

$\Rightarrow \quad x = \dfrac{1498 \times 100}{107} = 1400$

17. (A)

Let number of deer be x.

$\therefore \quad \dfrac{x}{2} + \dfrac{3}{4} \text{ of } \dfrac{x}{2} + 9 = x$

$\Rightarrow \quad \dfrac{x}{2} + \dfrac{3x}{8} + 9 = x$

$\Rightarrow \quad 4x + 3x + 72 = 8x$

$\Rightarrow \quad x = 72$

18. (A)

Let Raju's age $= 5x$.

$\therefore$ Rajan 's age $= 8x$

$\therefore \quad 5x + 5 = 8x - 4$

$\Rightarrow \quad 3x = 9 \Rightarrow x = 3$

Raju's age $= 5 \times 3 = 15$ years

19. (A)

Let the number be x.

$\therefore \quad 8\left(x - \dfrac{1}{2}\right) = 12 \Rightarrow 8x - 4 = 12$

$\Rightarrow \quad 8x = 16$

$\Rightarrow \quad x = 2$

20. (D)

Let distance of total journey be x km.

$\dfrac{x}{8} + \dfrac{x}{4} + \dfrac{3x}{5} + 8 = x$

$\Rightarrow \dfrac{5x + 10x + 24x + 320}{40} = x$

$\Rightarrow \quad 39x + 320 = 40x$

$\Rightarrow \quad x = 320$

HOTS (ACHIEVERS SECTION)

21. (D)	22. (C)	23. (C)	24. (B)	25. (C)

Answer Key

1. (D)	2. (B)	3. (B)	4. (B)	5. (A)	6. (B)	7. (A)	8. (C)	9. (D)	10. (C)
11. (D)	12. (A)	13. (A)	14. (C)	15. (B)	16. (A)	17. (B)	18. (C)	19. (C)	20. (A)

1. (D)

2. (B)

Let $\angle A$ be the smallest angle.

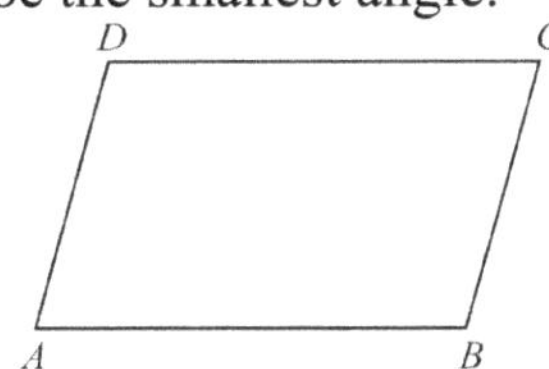

Let measure of $\angle A$ be $x°$.

$\therefore \qquad \angle C = x°$

$\therefore \qquad \angle D = \angle B = (2x - 24)°$

$\Rightarrow x° + (2x - 24)° = 180°$

$$\Rightarrow \quad x = \frac{(180 + 24)°}{3} = \frac{204}{3} = 68°$$

$\therefore$ largest angle of parallelogram

$$= (2 \times 68° - 24°)$$

$$= (136° - 24°) = 112°$$

3. (B)

The opposite sides of parallelogram are equal.

$\therefore \qquad 4x + 3x + 4x + 3x = 56$

$\Rightarrow \qquad 14x = 56 \Rightarrow x = 4$

$\therefore \qquad 4x = 4 \times 4 = 16$

and $3x = 4 \times 3 = 12$

$\therefore$ Difference $= 16 - 12 = 4$ cm

4. (B)

In rhombus $ABCD$,

$\angle DAB = 110° = \angle BCD$

$\angle DMC = 90°$

$$\angle DCM = \frac{1}{2} \times 110 = 55°$$

$\angle BDC = 180° - (90° + 55°)$

$\qquad = 180° - 145° = 35°$

5. (A)

Perimeter of parallelogram

$\qquad = 5 + 7 + 5 + 7 = 24$ cm

6. (B)

Let smaller side be x.

Longer side $= x + 3$

$\therefore \quad x + x + 3 + x + x + 3 = 36$

$\Rightarrow \quad 4x + 6 = 36 \Rightarrow 4x = 30$

$$\Rightarrow \qquad x = \frac{30}{4} = 7.5$$

7. (A)

$\because ABCD$ is a rhombus.

$\therefore \quad AB = BC = CD = DA$

$\because$ Diagonals of a rhombus bisect each other.

$$\therefore \quad AO = \frac{AC}{2} = \frac{24}{2} = 12 \text{ cm}$$

$$BO = \frac{BD}{2} = \frac{10}{2} = 5 \text{ cm}$$

$$\therefore \qquad AB = \sqrt{AO^2 + BO^2}$$

$$= \sqrt{12^2 + 5^2}$$

$$= \sqrt{144 + 25}$$

$$= \sqrt{169}$$

$$= 13$$

$\therefore \qquad BC = 10$ cm.

8. (C)

Given $BE = EC$

$\therefore \ \angle EBC = \angle ECB$

In $\triangle BEC$,

$2\angle EBC + \angle BEC = 180°$

$\Rightarrow \angle EBC = \angle ECB = 60°$

$\therefore \triangle EBC$ is an equilateral triangle having

$EB = BC = EC$

$AB = BC = CD = DA = EB = EC$

$[\because ABCD$ is a square$]$.

$\angle ABE = 90° + 60° = 150°$

In $\triangle ABE$,

$\angle ABE + 2\angle AEB = 180°$ $[\because \angle AEB = \angle BAE]$.

$2\angle AEB = 180° - \angle ABE = 180 - 150 = 30°$

$\Rightarrow \angle AEB = 15°$

9. **(D)**

$\angle ABC + \angle BCF = 180°$

[Interior angles or same side of transversal].

$\Rightarrow \angle BCF = 180° - 120° = 60°$

$\angle BCF = \angle EFD$ (corresponding angles)

$\therefore \angle EFD = 60°$

10. **(C)**

Joining A to C,

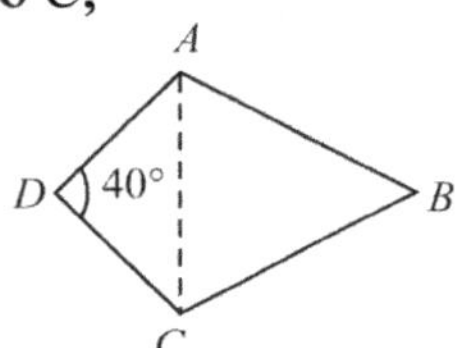

$\Rightarrow AD = DC$

$\therefore \angle DAC = DCA = \dfrac{180° - 40°}{2} = \dfrac{140}{2} = 70°$

$\because \angle BCD = 140°$ (given)

$\therefore \angle BCA = 140° - 70° = 70°$

Now, $\angle BCA = \angle BAC = 70°$ $(\because AB = BC)$

$\therefore \quad \angle ABC = 180° - (2 \times 70°)$

$= 180 - 140 = 40°$

11. **(D)**

In a parallelogram.

$AB = CD$, and, $BC = DA$

$\Rightarrow 3x + 1 = 25$ and $2y + 3 = y + 28$

$\Rightarrow \qquad x = 8$, and, $y = 25$

$\therefore \qquad x + y = 8 + 25 = 33$

12. **(A)**

$PQRS$ is a parallelogram.

$\therefore \qquad \angle S = \angle Q = y = 70°$

13. **(A)**

$\because \angle B = 90°$, and, $ABCD$ is a parallelogram

$\therefore \angle C = 90°$, $\angle A = 90°$ and $\angle D = 90°$

So, $ABCD$ may be a rectangle or square, but, since, $\alpha < 90°$.

$\therefore ABCD$ must be a rectangle.

14. **(C)**

$\because \theta = 90°$ (Angle between the diagonals)

$\therefore ABCD$ may be a rhombus or square.

But, since, $\angle A = \angle C = 110°$

$\therefore ABCD$ must be a rhombus.

15. **(B)**

$\because ABCD$ is an isosceles trapezium.

$\therefore \quad AD = BC$

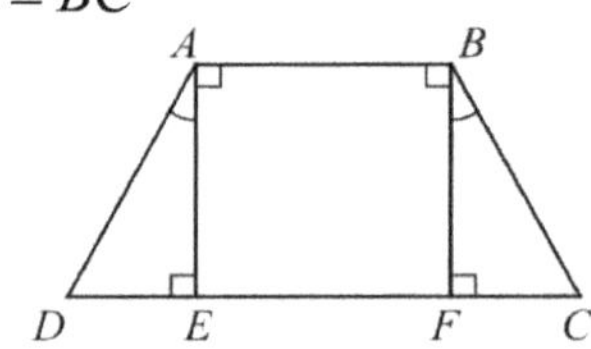

Draw $AE \perp DC$ and $BF \perp DC$, then, in $\triangle AED$ and $\angle BFC$.

$\angle AED = \angle BFC = 90°$,

$AD = BC$,

$AE = BF$ (perpendicular distance between two parallel lines)

$\therefore \quad \triangle AEB \cong \triangle BFC$ (ets congruency)

$\therefore \quad \angle A = \angle B$

16. **(A)**

$\because O$ is the bisector of both the diagonals.

$\therefore PQRS$ is a parallelogram.

$\because$ Diagonals of the parallelogram are equal.

$\therefore PQRS$ may be a square or rectangle.

17. **(B)**

$\because AB$ is parallel to BC, and, AB is transversal.

$\therefore \quad \angle A + \angle B = 180°$

$\Rightarrow \angle B = 180° - \angle A = 180° - 110° = 70°$

18. **(C)**

In $\triangle LAM$,

$\angle ALM + 90° + \angle M = 180°$

$\Rightarrow \angle M = 65°$

$\therefore x = \angle M = 60°$ $(\because KLMN$ is a parallelogram$)$.

In $\triangle BLK$,

$$\angle BLK + 65° + 90° = 180°$$
$$\Rightarrow \angle M = 180° - 90° = 90°$$
$$\Rightarrow \angle BLK = 25°$$
$$\because \quad \angle L = 180° - 65° = y + 25° + 25°$$
$$\Rightarrow y = 65°$$

19. (C)

$$\angle OBC = \angle ODA = 35°$$

(Alternate Interior $\angle S$).

20. (A)

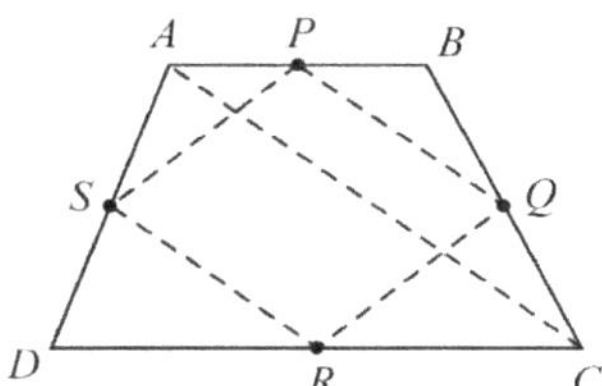

$ABCD$ is a parallelogram and P,Q,R,S are the midpoints of AB, BC, CD, DA respectively.

Consider, AC as a diagonal of $ABCD$.

Now, According to midpoint theorem,

$$PQ = \frac{1}{2} AC \text{ and } SR \text{ is parallel to AC,}$$

and $SR = \dfrac{1}{2} AC$ and SR is parallel to AC.

$\therefore PQ = RS$ and $PQ \parallel RS \parallel AC$.

$\therefore PQRS$ will be a parallelogram.

<table>
<tr><td colspan="5">HOTS (ACHIEVERS SECTION)</td></tr>
<tr><td>21. (C)</td><td>22. (B)</td><td>23. (B)</td><td>24. (A)</td><td>25. (C)</td></tr>
</table>

4. PRACTICAL GEOMETRY

Answer Key

1. (A)	2. (B)	3. (A)	4. (B)	5. (A)	6. (D)	7. (C)	8. (C)	9. (A)	10. (D)
11. (C)	12. (B)	13. (A)	14. (C)	15. (B)	16. (D)	17. (B)	18. (D)	19. (D)	20. (B)

1. (A)

A parallelogram is a simple quadrilateral with two pairs of parallel sides. The opposite sides of a parallelogram are parallel an equal in length.

2. (B)

Polygons that does not have any portion of diagonals in the exterior of polygon are called Convex Polygons.

3. (A)

As we know a polygon is a closed loop formed by line segments. So, to form a closed loop, minimum 3 sides are required and a polygon with 3 sides is known as triangle. Thus, a polygon with minimum number of sides is Triangle.

4. (B)

Polygons are a simple closed curves made up of line segments of equal lengths.

5. (A)

A Polygon is defined as a plane figure that is bounded by a finite chain of straight line segments closing in a loop to form a closed polygon chain.

6. (D)

Let, the two different sides of park be 'a' m and 'b' m respectively.

Given that, Parallelogram of park = 90m

$$\Rightarrow 2(a + b) = 90 \text{ m}$$
$$\Rightarrow a + b = 45 \text{ m} \qquad \text{...(i)}$$

Also, it is given that, one side is more than other by 10m, i.e.

$a = b + 10$ ...(ii)

From eq. (i) & (ii), we get, $b + 10 + b = 45$ m

$\Rightarrow 2b = 35$ m

$\Rightarrow b = 17.5$ m

Putting the value of b in eq. (ii), we get, $a = 17.5 + 10 = 27.5$ m

Thus, the four sides of the park are 17.5 m, 17.5 m, 27.5 m, 27.5 m.

7. (C)

Let, two adjacent sides of a parallelogram be of length 'a' cm and 'b' cm respectively. Given that , Perimeter of parallelogram = 72 cm

$\Rightarrow 2(a + b) = 72$cm

$\Rightarrow a + b = 36$ cm ...(i)

Also, It is given that, $a : b = 4 : 5$

$\Rightarrow a = 4/5b$ ...(ii)

From eq. (i) & (ii), we get, $4/5b + b = 36$ cm

$\Rightarrow 4b + 5b = 180$ cm

$\Rightarrow 9b = 180$ cm

$\Rightarrow b = 20$ cm putting value of b in eq. (ii), we get, $a = 16$ cm. Thus, two adjacent sides of parallelogram are 20cm, 16cm.

8. (C)

A square is a regular quadrilateral which has four equal sides and equal angles each of 900. The diagonals of a square are also equal and bisect each other at 90°.

9. (A)

As we know that, the sides of a regular polygon are equal and also we know, the angles opposite to equal sides are equal. So, all the angles of a polygon are of equal measure.

10. (D)

As we know that, the sum of the three interior angles of a triangle is 180°. In a right angle triangle, one angle will be of 90°. Thus, the remaining two angles should have sum of 90°. So, any other angle can not be of 90°. That's why, the maximum number of right angles in a right angle triangle is 1.

11. (C)

Step III is incorrect since with D as centre CD is drawn with radius = 4.4 cm.

15. (B)

To construct a quadrilateral, knowledge of at least five elements is necessary.

16. (D)

The correct step is : At C, $\angle ACD=120°$ draw such that CZ meets AX at D.

17. (B)

Here, it is given that AD + DC < AC which does not satisfy triangle inequality and hence quadrilateral cannot be drawn.

18. (D)

To construct a quadrilateral measure of at least five parts is necessary. In case of quadrilateral ABCD, if length of AB. BC and measure of $\angle A$, $\angle B$, $\angle C$ is required.

20. (B)

If the quadrilateral is irregular i.e it is not a rhombus or a parallelogram, then we need to know the lengths of all four sides plus one diagonal (i.e. at least five parts).

Example: For a quadrilateral ABCD, if we know AB = a, BC = b, CD = c, DA = d and AC = k then we can construct the unique parallelogram subjected that

$a + b > k$ and $c + d > k$.

In fact we would construct two triangles Δ ABC and Δ ADC on common base AC, apexes B and D being on either side of AC, using SSS method.

HOTS (ACHIEVERS SECTION)

| 21. (D) | 22. (A) | 23. (B) | 24. (A) | 25. (A) |

21. (D)

To construct a unique quadrilateral, we will need a minimum of 5 dimensions.

Here in option A, only four dimensions are provided, so a unique quadrilateral not possible because we don't know its angles.

In option B, we have five dimensions, but it does not result in a unique quadrilateral. we needed one more side length to construct uniquely.

In option C, It is not possible to construct a unique quadrilateral from only two diagonals given, unless it is a rhombus or square.

In option D, we have five dimensions. Here if we draw a side first then mark the angle on both ends then we can construct a quadrilateral uniquely.

Hence option D is correct.

22. (A)

No, it is not possible to construct a rhombus with diagonals equal to its sides.

It can be constructed only if one of the diagonals is equal. However, if both diagonals are equal, it's not possible.

We can assume two equilateral triangles on both sides of line segment AC with common base as AC.

Here, AB = AC, this implies that side AB is equal to diagonal AC, but if you look at another diagonal BD, it does not come out to be same.

Hence, its not possible to have both the diagonals equal to its sides.

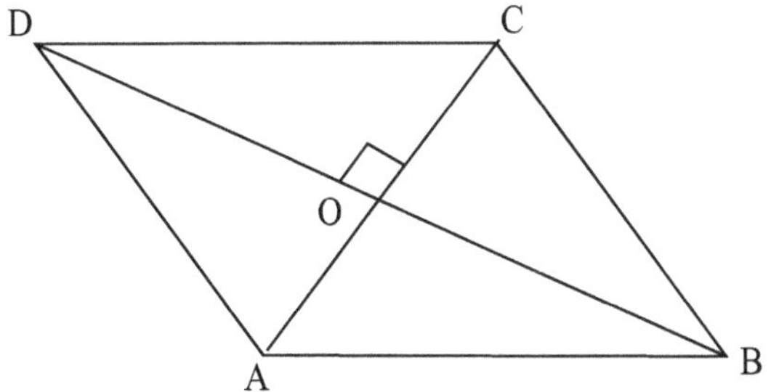

23. (B)

If we know the side only, we can't construct a unique rhombus because specific angles will be required to construct it, or if all angles are given, then also we can't construct a unique rhombus because a side length will be required to construct it.

But if the diagonals of rhombus are given we can construct a complete uniques rhombus. Here are the steps:

- Draw a diagonal AC.
- Draw a perpendicular bisector of AC, let the perpendicular bisector and AC intersects at O (as Diagonals of rhombus intersects at right angle)
- Taking O as centre and half of the length of another diagonal as radius, mark arc on the perpendicular bisector at both sides of AC. Name these intersection points as B and D
- Join AB, AD, BC, CD.
- ABCD is the required rhombus.

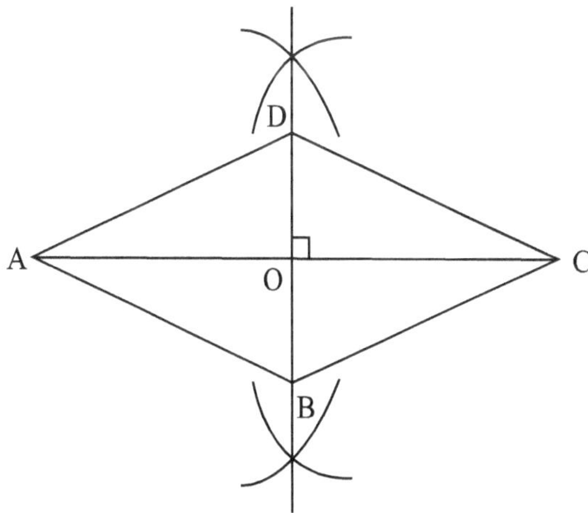

24. (A)

AB=BC=CD=AD and

AD∥BC, AB∥DC

All sides have equal length. Opposite sides are parallel, and opposite angles are equal, its a Rhombus.

25. (A)

Steps:

1. Draw a straight line AB of length 7.2cm
2. Draw perpendicular lines at A and B using protractor.
3. Using compass cut arc at the perpendicular from A and B of lengths 6cm
4. Join these cuts with a line CD as shown in figure.
5. Now measure the lengths of AC and BD.

We get that the length of AC is approx. 9.37 cm which is same as length of BD

Hence, AC = BD.

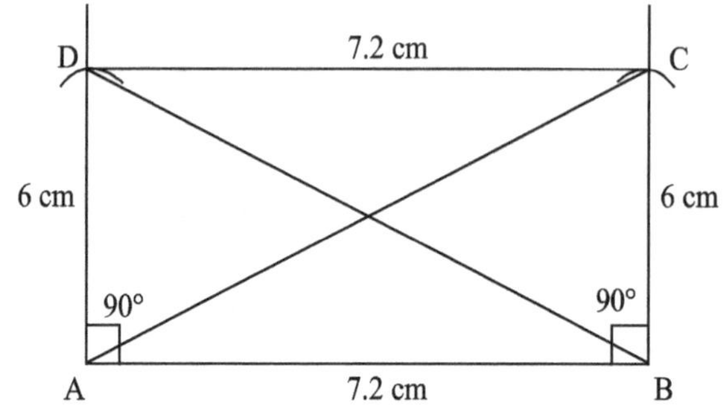

5. DATA HANDLING

Answer Key

1. (C)	2. (A)	3. (B)	4. (D)	5. (C)	6. (B)	7. (B)	8. (A)	9. (C)	10. (C)
11. (D)	12. (A)	13. (D)	14. (B)	15. (C)	16. (B)	17. (B)	18. (A)	19. (A)	20. (B)

1. (C)

Total number of all possible outcomes = 52

No. of diamonds = 13

P(getting a diamond) $= \dfrac{13}{52} = \dfrac{1}{4}$

2. (A)

Total number of balls = 4 + 5 + 7 = 16

Number of black balls = 7

P(getting a black ball) $= \dfrac{7}{16}$

3. (B)

Total production = 57 + 76 + 19 + 38 = 190

Central angle for rice $= \dfrac{57}{190} \times 360$

$= \dfrac{3}{10} \times 360 = 108°$

4. (D)

Amount of bill (₹)	300-400	400-500	500-600	600-700	700-800
Frequency	5	3	6	3	7

Frequency of the group = 700 – 800 = 7

5. (C)

Central angle

$= \dfrac{\text{Value of componeent}}{\text{Total value}} \times 360°$

$\Rightarrow \quad 100° = \dfrac{x}{14400} \times 360$

$\Rightarrow \quad x = \dfrac{100 \times 14400}{360} = ₹\,4000$

6. (B)

Percentage of cement $= \dfrac{72°}{360°} \times 100$

$= 20\%$

7. (B)

Total no. of tickets = 10 + 20 = 30

No. of blank tickets = 20

P(not getting a prize) $= \dfrac{20}{30} = \dfrac{2}{3}$

8. **(A)**
   Total no. of possible outcomes $= 52$
   Number of red cards $= 26$.

   $P(\text{getting a red card}) = \dfrac{26}{52} = \dfrac{1}{2}$

9. **(C)**
   Total no. of electric bulbs $= 100$
   No. of defective bulbs $= 8$
   No. of bulbs which are not defective
   $= 100 - 8 = 92$

   $P(\text{getting bulb is not defective}) = \dfrac{92}{100} = \dfrac{23}{25}$

10. **(C)**
   Total no. of possible outcomes $= 52$
   No. of queen $= 4$.

   $P(\text{getting a queen}) = \dfrac{4}{52} = \dfrac{1}{13}$

11. **(D)**
   Total no. of possible outcomes $= 6$

   $P(\text{getting 6}) = \dfrac{1}{6}$

12. **(A)**
   Total no. of possible outcomes $= 52$
   There are only 26 black cards (Clubs and 1 Spade)
   So the card of black can be taken out from 26

   $(\text{black 6 card}) = \dfrac{2}{52} = \dfrac{1}{26}$

13. **(D)**

Age	13-14	15-16	17-18
No. of members	22	18	10

   Percentage of members of 15-16 age group
   $= \dfrac{18}{50} \times 100 = 36\%$

14. **(B)**

   Amount spent on cricket $= \dfrac{150°}{360°} \times 10800$
   $= ₹\ 4500$

15. **(C)**

   Central angle for house rent $= \dfrac{20}{100} \times 360$
   $= 72°$

16. **(B)**
   Total no. of letters $= 7$
   no. of letter $S = 2$

   Probability that the letter is $S = \dfrac{2}{7}$

17. **(B)**
   Total no. of letters $= 8$
   No. of letter M $= 2$

   $P(\text{getting a letter M}) = \dfrac{2}{8} = \dfrac{1}{4}$

18. **(A)**
   Total no. of possible outcomes $= 8$
   Total no. of even numbers $= 4$

   $P(\text{getting an even number}) = \dfrac{4}{8} = \dfrac{1}{2}$

19. **(A)**
   Total no. of families $= 400$
   No. of families having 3 children $= 95$

   $P(\text{family having 3 children}) = \dfrac{95}{400} = \dfrac{19}{80}$

HOTS (ACHIEVERS SECTION)

21. (B)	22. (D)	23. (C)	24. (D)	25. (C)

Answer Key

1. (D)	2. (B)	3. (C)	4. (D)	5. (B)	6. (A)	7. (C)	8. (A)	9. (D)	10. (D)
11. (D)	12. (D)	13. (A)	14. (B)	15. (C)	16. (C)	17. (C)	18. (C)	19. (C)	20. (B)

1. (D)

$\Rightarrow$ Given $\sqrt{\dfrac{2x-1}{3}} = 5$

$\dfrac{2x-1}{3} = 25$

$\Rightarrow \quad 2x - 1 = 75 \Rightarrow 2x = 76 \Rightarrow x = \dfrac{76}{2} = 38$

2. (B)

The greatest number of five digits

$= 99999$

$$
\begin{array}{r|l|l}
3 & \overline{9}\;\overline{99}\;\overline{99} & 316 \\
3 & 9 & \\
\hline
61 & \times\,99 & \\
1 & 61 & \\
\hline
626 & 3899 & \\
6 & 3756 & \\
\hline
632 & \times\,143 & \\
\end{array}
$$

$\therefore$ Required number $= 99999 - 143 = 99856$

3. (C)

$$
\begin{array}{r|l|l}
8 & \overline{64}\;\overline{59} & 8 \\
8 & 64 & \\
\hline
16 & \times\times\times\times & \\
\end{array}
$$

$\therefore$ Required number $= 6459 - 59 = 6400$

Hence 59 must be subtracted.

4. (D)

$$
\begin{array}{r|l}
2 & 384 \\
2 & 192 \\
2 & 96 \\
2 & 48 \\
2 & 24 \\
2 & 12 \\
2 & 6 \\
\hline
 & 3 \\
\end{array}
$$

$\therefore 384 = \underline{2 \times 2} \times \underline{2 \times 2} \times \underline{2 \times 2} \times 2 \times 3$

$\therefore$ Required number $= 6$

5. (B)

Consider option (b)

$$
\begin{array}{r|l}
2 & 1024 \\
2 & 512 \\
2 & 256 \\
2 & 128 \\
2 & 64 \\
2 & 32 \\
2 & 16 \\
2 & 8 \\
2 & 4 \\
\hline
 & 2 \\
\end{array}
$$

Here $1024 = (2 \times 2) \times (2 \times 2) \times (2 \times 2)$
$\times (2 \times 2) \times (2 \times 2)$

Clearly 1024 is the smallest number of four digits which is a perfect square.

6. (A)

Greatest number of four digits $= 9999$

$$
\begin{array}{r|l|l}
9 & \overline{99}\;\overline{99} & 99 \\
9 & 81 & \\
\hline
189 & 18\;99 & \\
9 & 17\;01 & \\
\hline
198 & \times 198 & \\
\end{array}
$$

$\therefore$ Required number $= 9999 - 198 = 9801$

7. (C)

$$
\begin{array}{r|l|l}
4 & \overline{22}\;\overline{92} & 47 \\
4 & 16 & \\
\hline
8 & \times 692 & \\
\end{array}
$$

$47^2 = 2209$

$48^2 = 2304$

Required number $= 2304 - 2292 = 12$

8. (A)

$557568 = 11^2 \times 2^2 \times 2^2 \times 2 \times 12^2$

Required number $= 2$

9. (D)

$396 = 2 \times 2 \times 3 \times 3 \times 11$

To make it a perfect square, 11 is multiplied to 396.

10. (D)

6203

$78 \times 78 = 6084$

$79 \times 79 = 6241$

$6241 - 6203 = 38$

38 must be added to 6203 to make it a perfect square.

11. **(D)**

Here LCM of 8, 15, 20 = 120.

and $120 = 2 \times 2 \times 2 \times 3 \times 5$

To make 120 a perfect square, it must be multiplied by $2 \times 3 \times 5 = 30$

$120 \times 30 = 3600$

12. **(D)**

$36 \times 36 = 1296$

$37 \times 37 = 1369$

69 must be added to 1300 to make it a perfect square.

13. **(A)**

Perimeter of an equilateral triangle

$= 4 + 4 + 4 = 12$ cm

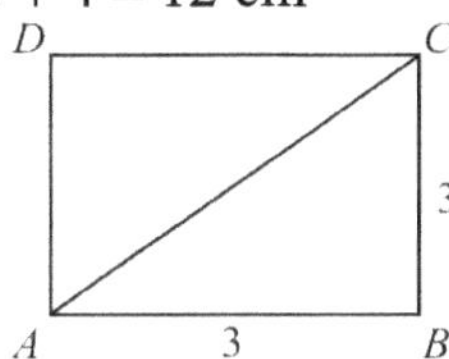

Perimeter of square = 12 cm

$\Rightarrow \qquad 4 \times$ side = 12

$\Rightarrow \qquad$ Side = 3 cm.

$\therefore$ Length of diagonal $= \sqrt{3^2 + 3^2}$

$= \sqrt{9 + 9}$

$= \sqrt{18} = 3\sqrt{2}$

$= 3 \times 1.414 = 4.24$ cm

14. **(B)**

Let the numbers are x and $3x$.

$\therefore \qquad x \times 3x = 29\dfrac{31}{49} = \dfrac{1452}{49}$

$\Rightarrow \qquad x^2 = \dfrac{1452}{49 \times 3} = \dfrac{484}{49} \Rightarrow x = \dfrac{22}{7}$

$\therefore \qquad 3x = 3 \times \dfrac{22}{7} = \dfrac{66}{7}$

15. **(C)**

Let breadth be x m

$\therefore$ Length = $3x$ m

Now $\quad x \times 3x = 348 \Rightarrow x^2 = \dfrac{348}{3} = 116$

$\Rightarrow \qquad x^2 = 116 \Rightarrow x = 10.77$

$\therefore \qquad 3x = 3 \times 10.77 = 32.31$

Perimeter = 2 (10.77 + 32.31) = 86.16 m

16. **(C)**

Here $3^2 + 4^2 = 5^2$

$6^2 + 8^2 = 10^2$

$2^2 + 3^2 \neq 4^2$

$12^2 + 35^2 = 37^2$

$\therefore$ (c) is not a Pythagorean triplet.

17. **(C)**

Speed of cycle = 18 km/hour

$= 18 \times \dfrac{5}{18} = 5$ m / sec

Area of square = 60025

Side of square $= \sqrt{60025} = 245$ m

Perimeter of square = 245 × 4 m

$\therefore$ Time taken $= \dfrac{245 \times 4}{5} = 196$ seconds

18. **(C)**

Area of square = Area of rectangle

$= 13.6 \times 3.4$

$= 46.24$

$\therefore$ Side of square $= \sqrt{46.24} = 6.8$ m

19. **(C)**

Perimeter of square = 76

$\Rightarrow 4 \times$ side = 76 $\Rightarrow$ side $= \dfrac{76}{4} = 19$

$\therefore$ Area of square $= 19^2 = 361$ m²

20. **(B)**

Here $729 = 27^2$, $324 = 18^2$,

$441 = 21^2$, $625 = 25^2$

or

Square of an odd number is an odd number.

HOTS (ACHIEVERS SECTION)

21. (A)	22. (B)	23. (B)	24. (B)	25. (B)

21. (A)

$x^2 + 6\sqrt{3}\,x - 48$

$= x^2 + 8\sqrt{3}x - 2\sqrt{3}x - 48$

$= x(x + 8\sqrt{3}) - 2\sqrt{3}\,(x + 8\sqrt{3})$

$= (x + 8\sqrt{3})\,(x - 2\sqrt{3})$

22. (B)

$\sqrt{0.0004} = 0.02$

23. (B)

$\sqrt{\dfrac{\frac{121}{100} \times \frac{9}{10}}{\frac{11}{10} \times \frac{11}{100}}} = \sqrt{\dfrac{121 \times 9}{11 \times 11}} = 3$

24. (B)

$\dfrac{\sqrt{0.2401} - \sqrt{0.1681}}{\sqrt{0.2401} + \sqrt{0.1681}}$

$\dfrac{49 - 41}{49 + 41} = \dfrac{8}{90} = \dfrac{4}{45}$

25. (B)

Area of square $= \dfrac{1}{2} \times (4\sqrt{2})^2$

$\qquad\qquad = \dfrac{1}{2} \times 16 \times 2 = 16\,\text{m}^2$

Side $= \sqrt{16} = 4$ m.

Perimeter $= 4 \times 4 = 16$ m.

7. CUBES AND CUBE ROOTS

Answer Key

1. (B)	2. (C)	3. (C)	4. (C)	5. (B)	6. (A)	7. (B)	8. (A)	9. (C)	10. (D)
11. (B)	12. (C)	13. (C)	14. (A)	15. (C)	16. (D)	17. (B)	18. (D)	19. (C)	20. (B)

1. **(B)**

Here $12^2 + 16^2 = 400$

$\therefore (\sqrt{12^2 + 16^2})^3 = (400)^{3/2} = (20)^3 = 8000$

2. **(C)**

$\left(\dfrac{64}{125}\right)^{2/3} = \left(\dfrac{4}{5}\right)^{3 \times \frac{2}{3}} = \left(\dfrac{4}{5}\right)^2 = \dfrac{16}{25}$

3. **(C)**

$(3n + 2)^3 = 27n^3 + 8 + 3 \times 3n \times 2(3n + 2)$

$= 27n^3 + 8 + 18n\,(3n + 2)$

$= 27n^3 + 54n^2 + 36n + 8$

$= 3\,(9n^3 + 18n^2 + 12n + 2) + 2 = 3n + 2$

4. **(C)**

If, $0 < p < 1$,

then, $p^3 < p$.

5. **(B)**

If, $p > 1$

then, $\qquad p - 1 > 0$

$\therefore \qquad\qquad p^3 > p$

6. **(A)**

Given $(2k)^3 + (3k)^3 + (4k)^3 = 2673$

$\Rightarrow \qquad\qquad 99\,k^3 = 2673$

$\Rightarrow \qquad\qquad k^3 = 27$

$\Rightarrow \qquad\qquad k = 3$

$\therefore$ Numbers are 6, 9, 12.

$\therefore$ Their sum $= 6 + 9 + 12 = 27$

7. **(B)**

$\sqrt[3]{\dfrac{4913}{343}} = \dfrac{17}{7}$

8. **(A)**

We have $(0.008)^{\frac{1}{3}} + (0.343)^{\frac{1}{3}} - (0.25)^{\frac{1}{2}}$

$\qquad\qquad = 0.2 + 0.7 - 0.5$

$\qquad\qquad = 0.9 - 0.5$

$\qquad\qquad = 0.4$

9. **(C)**

513 is not a perfect cube.

10. (D)

$4.2m = (74.088m^3)^{1/3}$

11. (B)

Here $3087 = 3 \times 3 \times 7 \times 7 \times 7 = 3^2 \times 7^3$.

$\because$ 3087 has two 3 as its factors, but one 3, is short to make 3087, a perfect cube.

$\therefore$ 3 should be multiplied to 3087 to produce a perfect cube.

12. (C)

$8788 = 2 \times 2 \times 13 \times 13 \times 13$.

$\therefore$ 8788 should be divided by (2×2), i.e., 4 to produce quotient as a perfect cube.

13. (C)

$392 = 2 \times 2 \times 2 \times 7 \times 7$

$\therefore$ 392 should be divided by (7×7), i.e., 49 to produce quotient, i.e., 8 as a perfect cube.

14. (A)

$2197 = 13^3$.

$\because$ The number, i.e., 2197 is odd.

$\therefore$ Its cube root should be odd.

15. (C)

$\because$ 1728 is even

$\therefore$ Its cube root should be even.

16. (D)

$343 = 7 \times 7 \times 7$

$\therefore$ 343 is a perfect cube.

17. (B)

$$\sqrt[3]{\frac{216}{2197}} = \left(\frac{6}{13}\right)^{3 \times \frac{1}{3}} = \frac{6}{13}$$

18. (D)

$x^3 y^2 = (3)^3 \times (-3)^2 = (3)^5 = 243$

19. (C)

$500 = 2 \times 2 \times 5 \times 5 \times 5 = 2^2 \times 5^3$

$\therefore 500 > 5^3$

$\therefore \quad 6^3 = 216,\ 7^3 = 343,\ 8^3 = 512$

$\therefore$ 12 should be added to make it a perfect cube.

20. (B)

$1370 = 2 \times 5 \times 137$

$1370 > 10^3 = 1000$

$\therefore \quad 11^3 = 1331,\ 12^3 = 1728$

$\therefore \qquad 1370 - 1331 = 39$

$\therefore$ Required number = 39

HOTS (ACHIEVERS SECTION)

21. (B)	22. (A)	23. (A)	24. (A)	25. (D)

8. COMPARING QUANTITIES

Answer Key

1. (A)	2. (A)	3. (B)	4. (A)	5. (A)	6. (B)	7. (C)	8. (B)	9. (A)	10 (B)
11. (A)	12. (A)	13. (D)	14. (B)	15. (B)	16. (B)	17. (B)	18. (C)	19. (C)	20. (D)
21. (A)	22. (B)	23. (C)	24. (A)	25. (A)					

1. **(A)**
Let the original price be ₹ x.

$\therefore \quad x + 8\% \text{ of } x = 180$

$\Rightarrow x + \dfrac{8x}{100} = 180$

$\Rightarrow \quad x = \dfrac{180 \times 100}{108} = ₹166.66$

2. **(A)**
C.P. of 1ˢᵗ cow

$= \dfrac{20,000 \times 100}{105} = 19047.62$

C.P. of 2ⁿᵈ cow $= \dfrac{20000 \times 100}{90} = 22222.22$

Total C.P. $= 19047.62 + 2222.22 = ₹41269.84$
Total S.P. $= ₹(20000 + 20000) = ₹40000$
Overall loss $= 41269.84 - 40000 = 1269.84$

3. **(B)**
Let the price of mobile before VAT be ₹ x.

$\therefore \quad x + 10\% \text{ of } x = 3300$

$\Rightarrow \quad x + \dfrac{10x}{100} = 3300$

$\Rightarrow \quad 11x = 3300 \times 10$

$\Rightarrow \quad x = \dfrac{3300 \times 10}{11} = 3000$

4. **(A)**
Let the marked price be ₹ x.

$\therefore \quad x - 5\% \text{ of } x = 5225$

$\Rightarrow \quad x - \dfrac{5x}{100} = 5225$

$\Rightarrow \quad 95x = 5225 \times 100$

$\Rightarrow \quad x = \dfrac{5225 \times 100}{95} = ₹5500$

5. **(A)**

We know $A = P\left(1 + \dfrac{R}{100}\right)^n$

$\therefore \quad A = 62500\left(1 + \dfrac{4}{100}\right)^3$

$= 62500 \times \dfrac{104}{100} \times \dfrac{104}{100} \times \dfrac{104}{100}$

$= 70304$

then C.I. $= 70304 - 62500 = 7804$

6. **(B)**
Value of scooter after one year

$= 42000\left(1 - \dfrac{8}{100}\right)^1$

$= 42000\left(\dfrac{100 - 8}{100}\right) = \dfrac{42000 \times 92}{100}$

$= \text{Rs. } 38640$

7. **(C)**
Let selling price of 20 pens $= ₹ 20$
$\therefore$ Now Gain $= ₹ 4$
Cost Price $= 20 - 4 = 16$

Hence Gain percent $= \dfrac{4}{16} \times 100 = 25\%$

8. **(B)**
Let the S.P. of 10 articles $= ₹ 10$

$\therefore$ S.P. of 1 article $= ₹ \dfrac{10}{10} = ₹ 1$

and C.P of 11 articles $= ₹ 10$

C.P of 1 article $= ₹ \dfrac{10}{11}$

$\therefore$ Gain $= 1 - \dfrac{10}{11} = \dfrac{1}{11}$

Hence Gain percent $= \dfrac{\frac{1}{11}}{\frac{10}{11}} \times 100$

$= \dfrac{1}{10} \times 100 = 10\%$

9. **(A)**
Let C.P. be ₹ x.
then $(x + 66) + 24\% \text{ of } (x + 66) = 7130$

$\Rightarrow \quad (x + 66) + \dfrac{24(x + 66)}{100} = 7130$

$\Rightarrow 100x + 6600 + 24x + 1584 = 713000$

$\Rightarrow \quad 124x = 713000 - 8184$

$\Rightarrow \quad 124x = 704816$

$\Rightarrow \quad x = \dfrac{704816}{124} = 5684$

10. **(B)**

Here Marked Price = ₹ 320.
and Discount = 10%
Selling Price = 320 – 10% of 320
$\quad$ = 320 – 32 = 288
Let C.P. be ₹ x.
$\therefore \qquad x + 20\% \text{ of } x = 288$

$$\Rightarrow \qquad x + \frac{20x}{100} = 288$$

$$x = \frac{288 \times 100}{120} = ₹ 240$$

11. (A)

Let the marked price = ₹ 100
and Discount = 20%
then price 100 – 20 = 80

$$2^{\text{nd}} \text{ Discount} = 10\% \text{ of } 80 = \frac{10 \times 80}{100} = 8$$

New price = 80 – 8 = 72
Successive discount = 100 – 72 = 28%

12. (A)

$$\text{Here } A = P\left(1 + \frac{r}{100}\right)^n$$

$$\Rightarrow 882 = 800\left(1 + \frac{5}{100}\right)^n$$

$$\Rightarrow \qquad \frac{882}{800} = \left(\frac{105}{100}\right)^n$$

$$\Rightarrow \qquad \frac{441}{400} = \left(\frac{21}{20}\right)^n$$

$$\Rightarrow \qquad \left(\frac{21}{20}\right)^2 = \left(\frac{21}{20}\right)^n$$

$$\Rightarrow \qquad n = 2$$

13. (D)

$$\text{We know } A = P\left(1 + \frac{r}{100}\right)^n.$$

Here $\qquad r = \dfrac{10}{2} = 5\%$

and $\qquad n = 2 \times 2 = 4$

$$\therefore \quad 9724.05 = P\left(1 + \frac{5}{100}\right)^4$$

$$\Rightarrow 9724.05 = P\left(\frac{100 + 5}{100}\right)^4$$

$$\Rightarrow 9724.05 = P\left(\frac{21}{20}\right)^4$$

$$\Rightarrow \qquad P = \frac{9724.05 \times 20 \times 20 \times 20 \times 20}{21 \times 21 \times 21 \times 21}$$

$$\Rightarrow \qquad P = \frac{9724.05 \times 400 \times 400}{441 \times 441} = 8000$$

14. (B)

$$\text{Here } A = P\left(1 + \frac{r}{100}\right)^n$$

$$\Rightarrow \qquad 2662 = 2000\left(1 + \frac{r}{100}\right)^3$$

$$\Rightarrow \qquad \frac{2662}{2000} = \left(1 + \frac{r}{100}\right)^3$$

$$\Rightarrow \qquad 1.331 = \left(1 + \frac{r}{100}\right)^3$$

$$\Rightarrow \qquad (1.1)^3 = \left(1 + \frac{r}{100}\right)^3$$

$$\Rightarrow \quad 1 + \frac{r}{100} = 1.1 \Rightarrow \frac{r}{100} = 0.1$$

$$\Rightarrow \qquad r = 0.1 \times 100 = 10\%$$

15. (B)

Let Marked Price = ₹ 100
First Discount = 20%
Price = 100 – 20 = 80.

$$\text{Second Discount} = 10\% \text{ of } 80 = \frac{10 \times 80}{100} = 8$$

Price after 2nd discount = $80 - 8 = 72$

Third Discount = 5% of $72 = \dfrac{5 \times 72}{100} = 3.6$

Price after 3rd discount = $72 - 3.6 = 68.4$

Single equivalent discount = $100 - 68.4$
$$= 31.6\%$$

16. (B)

Selling Price = $3300 \times \dfrac{110}{100} = 3000$

Let Marked Price be ₹ x

$x - 20\%$ of $\Rightarrow x = x - \dfrac{20x}{100} = \dfrac{80x}{100}$

$$\dfrac{80x}{100} = 3300$$

$\Rightarrow \qquad x = \dfrac{100 \times 3300}{80} = 4125$

17. (B)

Let the price be ₹ x.

then $x + 6\%$ of $x = 53$

$\Rightarrow \qquad x + \dfrac{6x}{100} = 53$

$\Rightarrow \qquad 106x = 53 \times 100$

$\Rightarrow \qquad x = \dfrac{53 \times 100}{106} = 50$

18. (C)

Let sales tax = $x\,\%$

$\Rightarrow\ 900 + x\%$ of $900 = 999$

$\Rightarrow 900 + \dfrac{900 \times x}{100} = 999$

$\Rightarrow 9x = 99 \Rightarrow x = 11$

19. (C)

Price = ₹ 1200

Increased Price = $1200 + 10\%$ of 1200
$$= 1200 + 120 = 1320$$

Discount = 15% of 1320

$= \dfrac{15 \times 1320}{100}$

$= 198$

The net payable amount = $1320 - 198$
$$= ₹1122$$

20. (D)

Here $A = P\left(1 + \dfrac{r}{100}\right)^n$

then $A = 8000\left(1 + \dfrac{10}{100}\right)^3$

$= 8000\left(\dfrac{110}{100}\right)^3$

$= 8000 \times \dfrac{110}{100} \times \dfrac{110}{100} \times \dfrac{110}{100}$

$= 8 \times 1331$

$= 10648$

21. (A)

Let the cost price be ₹ 100

Marked price = ₹ 140

Discount = 25% of $140 = \dfrac{25 \times 140}{100} = 35$

Selling price = $140 - 35 = 105$

Gain Percent = $105 - 100 = 5\%$

22. (B)

Let the cost price of 12 books = ₹ x.

Cost price of 1 book $= \dfrac{x}{12}$

Selling price of 15 books = ₹ x.

S.P. of 1 book $= \dfrac{x}{15}$

$\therefore \qquad \dfrac{x}{12} - \dfrac{x}{15} = \dfrac{5x - 4x}{60} = \dfrac{x}{60}$

Loss percent = $x/60 \div x/12 \times 100$

$= \dfrac{x}{60} \times \dfrac{12}{x} \times 100$

$= 20\%$

23. (C)

Here $A = P\left(1 + \dfrac{r}{100}\right)^n$

$$\Rightarrow A = 10000\left(1 + \dfrac{10}{100}\right)^3$$

$$= 10000 \times \dfrac{110}{100} \times \dfrac{110}{100} \times \dfrac{110}{100}$$

$$= 10 \times 1331 = 13310$$

$$\text{C.I.} = A - P = 13310 - 10000 = ₹\,3310$$

24. **(A)**

Let the purchase price $= ₹\, x$

then

$$4000 = x\left(1 - \dfrac{20}{100}\right)^2$$

$$\Rightarrow \quad 4000 = x\left(\dfrac{80}{100}\right)^2$$

$$\Rightarrow \quad x = \dfrac{4000 \times 100 \times 100}{80 \times 80}$$

$$\Rightarrow \quad x = 6250$$

25. **(A)**

Let sum $= ₹\,$ P.

then $\text{S.I.} = \dfrac{P \times r \times t}{100}$

$$\Rightarrow \quad 1200 = \dfrac{P \times 5 \times 3}{100}$$

$$\Rightarrow \quad P = \dfrac{1200 \times 100}{5 \times 3} = 8000$$

$$\Rightarrow \quad A = 8000\left(1 + \dfrac{5}{100}\right)^3$$

$$= 8000 \times \dfrac{105}{100} \times \dfrac{105}{100} \times \dfrac{105}{100} = ₹\,9261$$

$$\therefore \quad \text{C.I.} = 9261 - 8000 = 1261$$

HOTS (ACHIEVERS SECTION)

26. (C)	27. (A)	28. (B)	29. (C)	30. (D)

9. ALGEBRAIC EXPRESSIONS AND THEIR IDENTITIES

Answer Key

1. (A)	2. (B)	3. (C)	4. (B)	5. (A)	6. (A)	7. (A)	8. (B)	9. (A)	10 (B)
11. (B)	12. (C)	13. (B)	14. (B)	15. (B)	16. (D)	17. (A)	18. (B)	19. (A)	20. (A)
21. (D)	22. (A)	23. (B)	24. (C)	25. (A)					

1. **(A)**

$(x + y)^2 = x^2 + y^2 + 2xy$

$x^2 + y^2 = (x + y)^2 - 2xy$

$$= (12)^2 - 2 \times 14$$

$$= 144 - 28$$

$$= 116$$

2. **(B)**

$$\left(x + \dfrac{1}{x}\right)^2 = x^2 + \dfrac{1}{x^2} + 2 \times x \times \dfrac{1}{x}$$

$$x^2 + \dfrac{1}{x^2} = (11)^2 - 2 = 121 - 2 = 119$$

3. **(C)**

$$(x + y)^2 = x^2 + y^2 + 2xy$$

$$x - y = \sqrt{(x + y)^2 - 4xy}$$

$$= \sqrt{(100^2 - 4 \times 9}$$

$$= \sqrt{100 - 36} = \sqrt{64} = 8$$

$$\therefore \quad (x + y)(x - y) = x^2 - y^2$$

$$x^2 - y^2 = 10 \times 8 = 80$$

4. (B)

$$x + \frac{1}{x} = 7$$

$$\left(x + \frac{1}{x}\right)^2 = 7^2 \Rightarrow x^2 + \frac{1}{x^2} = 49 - 2 = 47$$

$$\left(x^2 + \frac{1}{x^2}\right)^2 = x^4 + \frac{1}{x^4} + 2$$

$$\Rightarrow \quad x^4 + \frac{1}{x^4} = (47)^2 - 2$$

$$= 2209 - 2 = 2207$$

5. (A)

Third side $= 6m^2 - 4m + 9$

$- (m^2 - 2m + 1 + 2m^2 + 3m + 5)$

$= 6m^2 - 4m + 9 - (3m^2 + m + 6)$

$= 6m^2 - 4m + 9 - 3m^2 - m - 6$

$= 3m^2 - 5m + 3$

6. (A)

$$
\begin{array}{r}
5x + 2 \\
x^2 - 3x + 4 \overline{)\ 5x^3 - 13x^2 + 15x + 7} \\
5x^3 - 15x^2 + 20x \\
\hline
2x^2 - 5x + 7 \\
2x^2 - 6x + 8 \\
\hline
x - 1
\end{array}
$$

Clearly $(x - 1)$ is remainder.

7. (A)

$$
\begin{array}{r}
x^2 - 3x + 4 \\
x^2 + x + 1 \overline{)\ x^4 - 2x^3 + 2x^2 + x + 4} \\
x^4 + x^3 + x^2 \\
\hline
-3x^3 + x^2 + x \\
-3x^3 - 3x^2 - 3x \\
\hline
4x^2 + 4x + 4 \\
4x^2 + 4x + 4 \\
\hline
\times \quad \times \quad \times
\end{array}
$$

$\therefore$ Quotient $= x^2 - 3x + 4$

8. (B)

$$
\begin{array}{r}
5x + 6 \\
x^2 - 2x + 3 \overline{)\ 5x^3 - 4x^2 + 3x + 18} \\
5x^3 - 10x^2 + 15x \\
\hline
6x^2 - 12x + 18 \\
6x^2 - 12x + 18 \\
\hline
\times \quad \times \quad \times
\end{array}
$$

9. (A)

$$x - \frac{1}{x} = 6$$

$$\Rightarrow \quad \left(x - \frac{1}{x}\right)^2 = 6^2$$

$$\Rightarrow \quad x^2 + \frac{1}{x^2} = 36 + 2 = 38$$

10. (B)

$$\frac{8\,a^2\,b^3}{-2ab} = -4ab^2$$

11. (B)

$$\frac{198 \times 198 - 102 \times 102}{96} = \frac{(198)^2 - (102)^2}{96}$$

$$= \frac{(198 + 102)(198 - 102)}{96} = \frac{300 \times 96}{96} = 300$$

12. (C)

$$(2abc)(-16\,a^2\,bc)(3a\,b^2\,c^2) = -96\,a^4\,b^4\,c^4$$

13. (B)

$$\because \quad x + \frac{1}{x} = 2$$

$$\Rightarrow \qquad x^2 + \frac{1}{x^2} = 4 - 2 = 2$$

and
$$x^4 + \frac{1}{x^4} = \left(x^2 + \frac{1}{x^2}\right)^2 - 2$$
$$= 2^2 - 2$$
$$= 4 - 2 = 2$$

14. (B) We have $\dfrac{8.37 \times 8.37 - 1.63 \times 1.63}{0.674}$

$$= \frac{(8.37)^2 - (1.63)^2}{0.674}$$

$$= \frac{(8.37 + 1.63)\,(8.37 - 1.63)}{0.674}$$

$$= \frac{10 \times 6.74}{0.674} = \frac{10 \times 674 \times 1000}{674 \times 100} = 100$$

15. (B)

$$\begin{array}{r}
3x + 2 \\
2x - 5 \overline{) \;6x^2 - 11x + 15\;} \\
6x^2 - 15x \\
\hline
4x + 15 \\
4x - 10 \\
\hline
25
\end{array}$$

16. (D)

$$\begin{array}{r}
5p^3 + p^2 \cdot \frac{26}{3} + \frac{25}{9}p + \frac{80}{27} \\
3p - 2 \overline{) \;15p^4 + 16p^3 - 9p^2 + 10/3p - 6\;} \\
15p^4 - 10p^3 \\
\hline
26p^3 - 9p^2 \\
26p^3 - \frac{52}{3}p^2 \\
\hline
\frac{25}{3}p^2 + \frac{10}{3}p \\
\frac{25}{3}p^2 - \frac{50}{9}p \\
\hline
\frac{80}{9} - 6 \\
\frac{80}{9} - \frac{160}{27} \\
\hline
\frac{-2}{27}
\end{array}$$

17. (A)
H.C.F. of $11abc^3$, $13a^2b^2c$, $17ab^3c^2 = abc$

18. (B)
$$x^2 - y^2 + 2yz - z^2$$
$$= x^2 - (y^2 - 2yz + z^2)$$
$$= x^2 - (y - z)^2$$
$$= (x + y - z)\,(x - y + z)$$

19. (A)

$$\begin{array}{r}
x^2 - x + 1 \\
x^2 + x + 1 \overline{) \;x^4 + x^2 + 1\;} \\
x^4 + x^3 + x^2 \\
\hline
- x^3 + 1 \\
- x^3 - x^2 - x \\
\hline
x^2 + x + 1 \\
x^2 + x + 1 \\
\hline
0
\end{array}$$

20. (A)
$$11a^2 + 54a + 63$$
$$= 11a^2 + 33a + 21a + 63$$
$$= 11a\,(a + 3) + 21\,(a + 3)$$
$$= (a + 3)\,(11a + 21)$$

21. (D)
$$1 - \frac{5}{3}x + 9x^2 - 6x^3 - x^4$$

Degree of the polynomial = Highest power of $x = 4$

22. (A)

$$\begin{array}{r}
x^2 + 2x + 4 \\
x^2 - 2x + 4 \overline{) \;x^4 + 4x^2 + 10\;} \\
x^4 - 2x^3 + 4x^2 \\
\hline
+ 2x^3 + 10 \\
2x^3 - 4x^2 + 8x \\
\hline
4x^2 - 8x + 10 \\
4x^2 - 8x + 16 \\
\hline
- 6
\end{array}$$

23. **(B)**

Clearly $x^2 + \sqrt{x} - 2 = 0$ is not a polynomial.

24. **(C)**

$$\frac{1}{4} x^2 y^2 z^2 \times 3x \times \frac{3}{2} y^2 z$$

$$= \frac{9}{8} x^3 y^4 z^3$$

25. **(A)**

$$\left(x - \frac{1}{x}\right)^2 = 36$$

$$\Rightarrow \quad x^2 + \frac{1}{x^2} = 36 + 2 = 38$$

$$\therefore \quad \left(x^2 + \frac{1}{x^2}\right)^2 = 38^2$$

$$x^4 + \frac{1}{x^4} = 38^2 - 2$$

$$= 1444 - 2$$

$$= 1442$$

HOTS (ACHIEVERS SECTION)

26. (D)	27. (A)	28. (A)	29. (A)	30. (C)

26. **(D)**

$$\frac{(x+3)(7-2x)}{(x+4)(5-x)} = 2$$

$$\Rightarrow \quad (x+3)(7-2x) = 2(x+4)(5-x)$$

$$\Rightarrow 7x - 2x^2 + 21 - 6x = 2(5x - x^2 + 20 - 4x)$$

$$\Rightarrow \quad x + 21 = 2x + 40$$

$$\Rightarrow \quad x = 21 - 40 = -19$$

27. **(A)**

$$9x^2 + 25 - 30x = (3x)^2 + (5)^2 - 2(3x)(5)$$

$$= (3x - 5)^2$$

28. **(A)**

$$x^2 + 17x + 60$$

$$= x^2 + 5x + 12x + 60 = x(x+5) + 12(x+5)$$

$$= (x+5)(x+12)$$

10. VISUALISING SOLID SHAPES

Answer Key

1. (C)	2. (A)	3. (B)	4. (B)	5. (B)	6. (C)	7. (A)	8. (B)	9. (D)	10 (C)
11. (B)	12. (D)	13. (A)	14. (B)	15. (D)	16. (B)	17. (A)	18. (B)	19. (C)	20. (C)
21. (B)	22. (B)	23. (D)	24. (B)	25. (C)					

1. **(C)**

Prism has congruent base and top faces and remaining faces are parallelograms.

2. **(A)**

A regular polyhedron has congruent face.

3. **(B)**

A cylinder has 2 circular and 1 lateral surface.

4. **(B)**

A tetrahedron has 4 equilateral triangles.

5. **(B)**

A hexahedron contains 6 squares.

6. **(C)**

A paraboloid can be generated by rotating a parabola about its axis.

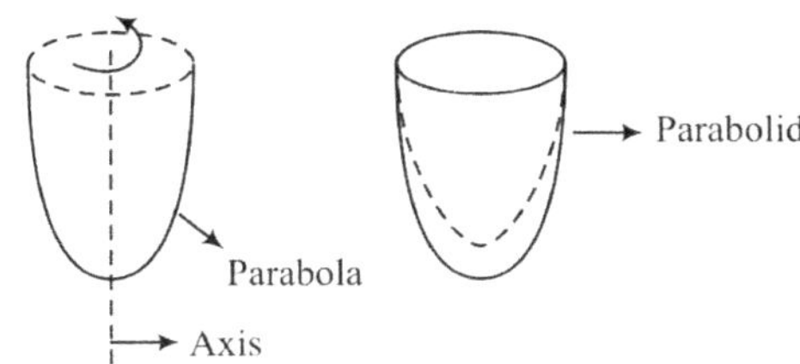

7. (A)

Number of faces $= F = 8$

Number of vertices $= V = 10$

$\therefore$ Using Euler's formula,

$E = V + F - 2 = 8 + 10 - 2 = 16$

8. (B)

A dodecahedron has 12 regular pentagons.

9. (D)

A isosahedron has 20 faces.

10. (C)

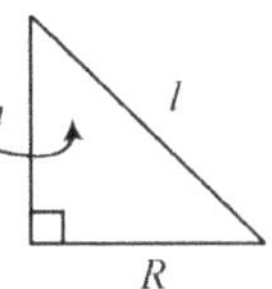
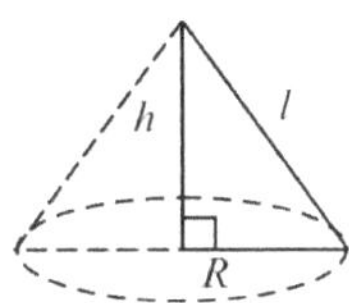

11. (B)

A hexahedron can be generated by sticking two equal tetrahedrons through their base.

12. (D)

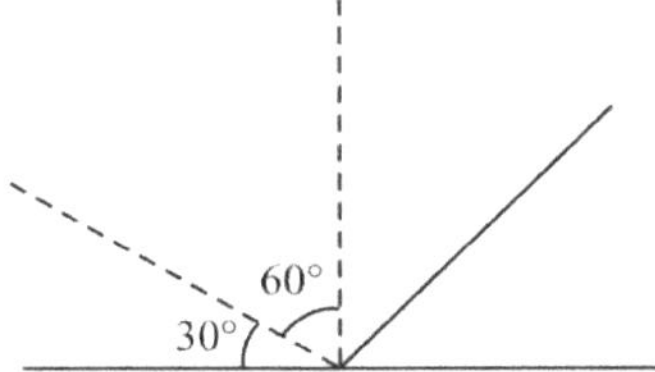

The edges are inclined at $30°$ to the horizontal and $60°$ to the vertical.

13. (A)

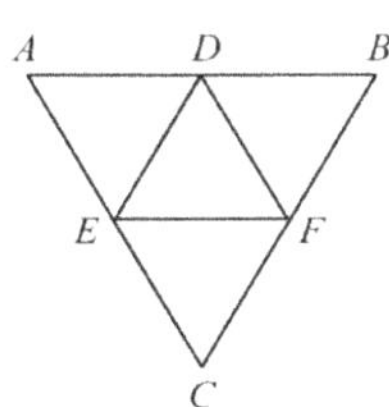

$AB = BC = AC$

$DE = EF = DF = \dfrac{BC}{2}$

[This is the front view of a tetrahedron]

14. (B)

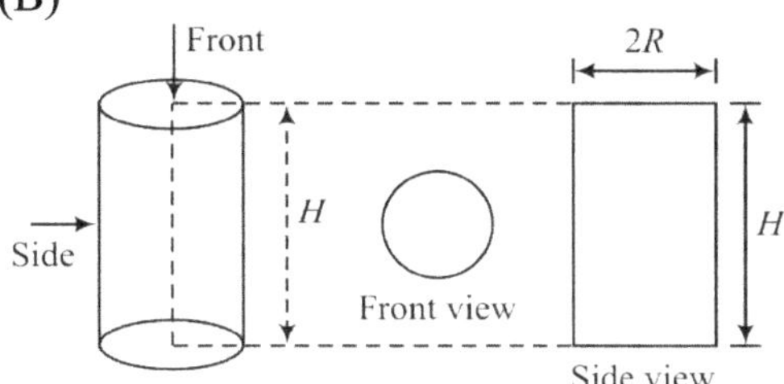

15. (D)

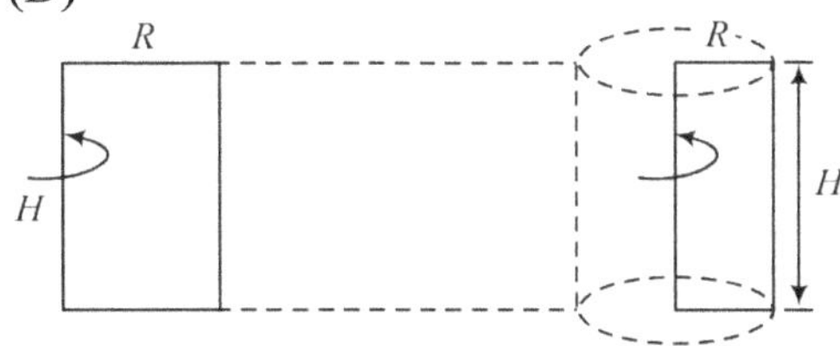

16. (B)

When we extrude a rectangle, a cuboid will be generated.

17. (A)

The top view will have 1 rectangle joined with a square.

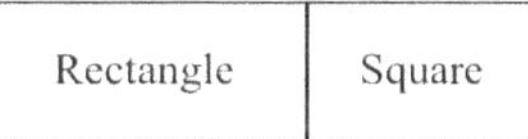

18. (B)

Number of squares in front view $= 3$

Number of squares in top view $= 3$

$\therefore\ x + y = (3 + 3) = 6$

19. (C)

Top view :

Number of edges $= 7$

20. (C)

When 2 cubes are joined, then the number of edges will be

$= (12 + 12) - (4) = 20$

When another cube is joined to the two cubes in desired manner then no. of edges

$= (20 + 12) - (4) = 28$

$\because$ cubes are of same dimensions.

21. (B)

After joining of 2 cubes, a cuboid will be formed,

$\therefore$ No. of vertices $= 8$

After final joining, no. of vertices
$= 8 + 4 = 12$

22. (B)

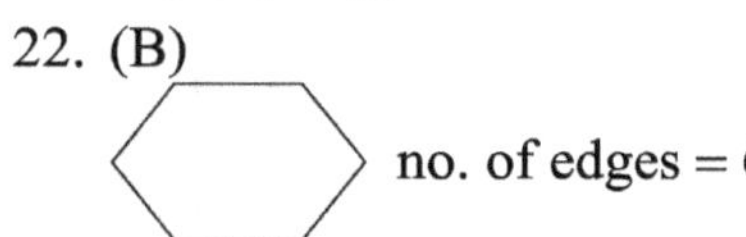

no. of edges $= 6$

23. (D)

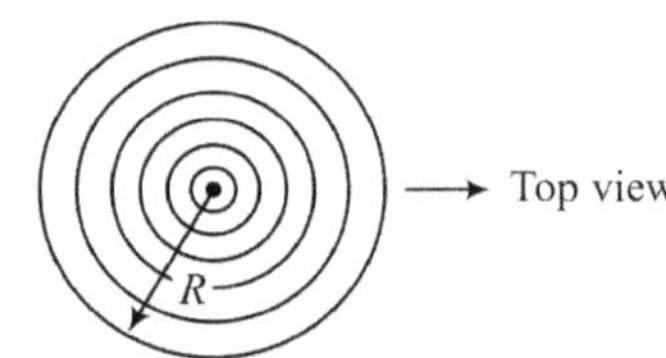

The top view of a cone contains circles with radii varying from zero to R, in radial directions (same centre)

24. (B)

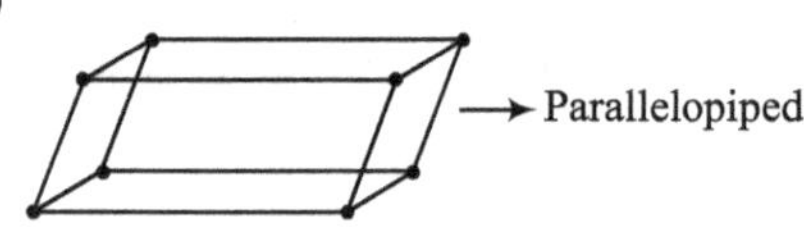

25. (C)

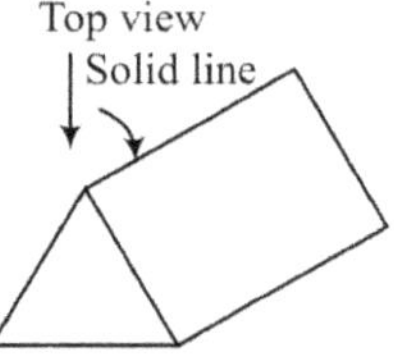

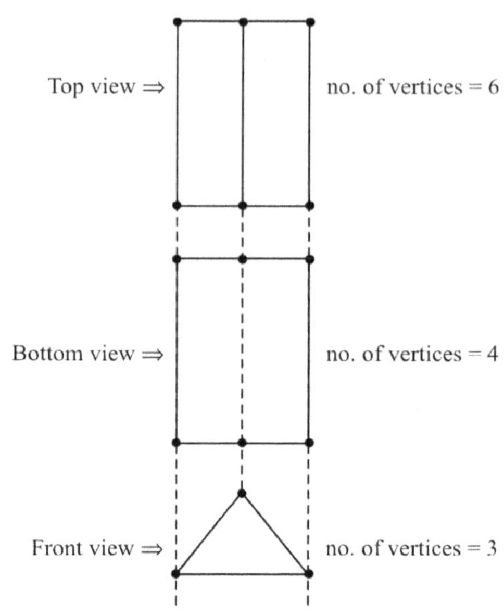

$\therefore$ Required no. of vertices $= (3 + 6) - (4) = 5$.

$\because$ Top view has solid line, but the solid line will be invisible in bottom view.

$\therefore$ Top view has 6 vertices and bottom view has 4 vertices.

<table>
<tr><td colspan="5">HOTS (ACHIEVERS SECTION)</td></tr>
<tr><td>26. (B)</td><td>27. (D)</td><td>28. (A)</td><td>29. (D)</td><td>30. (A)</td></tr>
</table>

11. MENSURATION

Answer Key

1. (C)	2. (B)	3. (A)	4. (C)	5. (A)	6. (C)	7. (D)	8. (A)	9. (B)	10 (A)
11. (B)	12. (B)	13. (B)	14. (C)	15. (B)	16. (C)	17. (C)	18. (A)	19. (B)	20. (A)
21. (B)	22. (A)	23. (A)	24. (B)	25. (C)					

1. (C)

Capacity of the tank $= 5632 \text{ m}^3$

Radius $= \dfrac{16}{2} = 8 \text{ m}$

Let its depth be h m.

$$\pi r^2 h = 5632$$

$\Rightarrow \quad \dfrac{22}{7} \times 8 \times 8h = 5632$

$\Rightarrow \quad h = \dfrac{5632 \times 7}{22 \times 8 \times 8} = 28\,m$

2. (B)

Volume of the cylinder = 1232 cm³

$\Rightarrow \quad \pi r^2 h = 1332$

$\Rightarrow \quad \dfrac{22}{7} \times r^2 \times 8 = 1232$

$\Rightarrow \quad r^2 = \dfrac{1232 \times 7}{8 \times 22}$

$\Rightarrow r^2 = 7 \times 7 \Rightarrow r = 7$ cm

Curved surface area $= 2\pi rh = 2 \times \dfrac{22}{7} \times 7 \times 8$

$= 352$ cm²

Total surface area

$= 2\pi r\,(h + r) = 2 \times \dfrac{22}{7} \times 7\,(8 + 7)$

$= 44 \times 15 = 660$ cm²

Difference = 660 − 352 = 308 cm²

3. (A)

Total surface area of cube = 486 cm²

$6a^2 = 486 \Rightarrow a^2 = 81$

$\Rightarrow \quad a = 9$

Volume of cube $= a^3 = 9^3 = 729$ cm³

4. (C)

Let x be the width of the beam.

Volume of the beam = 1.35 m³

$\Rightarrow \quad l \times b \times h = 1.35$

$\Rightarrow \quad x = \dfrac{1.35 \times 100}{5 \times 36}$

$\Rightarrow \quad x = \dfrac{135}{5 \times 36} = \dfrac{27}{36}\,m$

$\Rightarrow \quad x = \dfrac{27}{36} \times 100 = 75$ cm

5. (A)

Number of planks $= \dfrac{5 \times 100 \times 70 \times 32}{2 \times 100 \times 25 \times 8}$

$= 28$

6. (C)

Let radius be $3x$ and height be $7x$

Volume of the cylinder $= \pi r^2 h = 1584$

$\Rightarrow \quad \dfrac{22}{7} \times 3x \times 3x \times 7x = 1584$

$\Rightarrow \quad x^3 = \dfrac{1584 \times 7}{22 \times 3 \times 3 \times 7}$

$\Rightarrow \quad x^3 = 8 = 2^3 \Rightarrow x = 2$

∴ Radius = $3x$ = 3 × 2 = 6 cm

7. (D)

Volume of the wall = 33 × 3.5 × 0.4

$= 33 \times 100 \times 3.5 \times 100 \times 0.4 \times 100$

$= 3300 \times 350 \times 40$

Sand $= \dfrac{1}{10} \times 3300 \times 350 \times 40$

$= 330 \times 350 \times 40$

Required volume

$= 3300 \times 350 \times 40 - 330 \times 350 \times 40$

$= 3300 \times 40\,(350 - 35)$

$= 3300 \times 40 \times 315$

∴ No. of bricks $= \dfrac{3300 \times 40 \times 315}{22 \times 10 \times 7}$

$= \dfrac{300 \times 4 \times 45}{2}$

$= 300 \times 2 \times 45 = 27000$

8. (A)

$2\pi r = 44 \Rightarrow r = \dfrac{44}{2\pi} = \dfrac{44 \times 7}{2 \times 22} = 7$ cm

$h = 18$ cm

∴ Volume of the cylinder $= \pi r^2 h$

$= \dfrac{22}{7} \times 7^2 \times 18$

$= 22 \times 7 \times 18 = 2772$ cm³

9. (B)

Volume of cone $= \dfrac{1}{3}\,(\pi r^2)\,(h)$

$= \dfrac{1}{3}\,$ (Area of base) (height)

$$= \frac{1}{3} \times 180 \text{ cm}^2 \times 8 \text{ cm}$$

$$= 480 \text{ cm}^3$$

10. (A)

Given, the radii of cylinder = 2 : 3.

Heights of cylinder = 5 : 3

$\therefore$ Ratio of volume of the cylinders

$$= \pi \times (2x)^2 \times 5x : \pi (3x)^2 \times 3x$$

$$= 4 \times 5 : 9 \times 3$$

$$= 20 : 27$$

12. (B)

Here $h = 6$ cm.

$$\Rightarrow 2\pi r = 22 \Rightarrow r = \frac{22}{2\pi} = \frac{22 \times 7}{2 \times 22} = \frac{7}{2} \text{ cm}$$

Volume of the cylinder $= \pi r^2 h$

$$= \frac{22}{7} \times \frac{7}{2} \times \frac{7}{2} \times 6$$

$$= 11 \times 7 \times 3 = 231 \text{ cm}^3$$

13. (B)

Lateral surface area = 11440.

$$\Rightarrow \qquad 2\pi r h = 11440$$

$$\Rightarrow 2 \times \frac{22}{7} \times r \times 65 = 11440$$

$$\Rightarrow \qquad r = \frac{11440 \times 7}{44 \times 65} = 28 \text{ cm}$$

Circumference $= 2\pi r$

$$= 2 \times \frac{22}{7} \times 28 = 22 \times 8 = 176 \text{ cm}$$

14. (C)

Width of section $AEFB$ = width of $CGHD$

$$= \frac{1}{2}(28 - 20) = \frac{8}{2} = 4 \text{ cm}$$

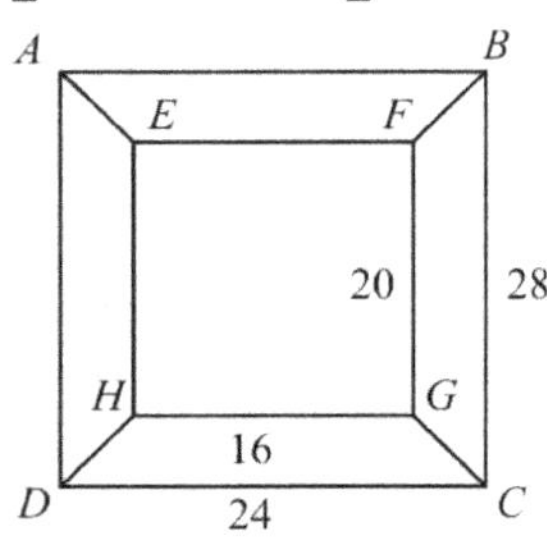

Area of $AEFB = \frac{1}{2} \times (24 + 16) \times 4 = 80 \text{ cm}^2$

Width of section $AEHD =$

width of $BFCG = \frac{1}{2}(24 - 16) = 4 \text{ cm}$

Area of $AEHD = \frac{1}{2} \times (28 + 20) \times 4 = 96 \text{ cm}^2$

Difference $= 96 - 80 = 16 \text{ cm}^2$

15. (B)

Area of trapezium $= \frac{1}{2} \times (20 + x)\,15$

$$\Rightarrow \qquad 480 = \frac{1}{2}(20 + x)\,15$$

$$\Rightarrow \quad 20 + x = \frac{2 \times 480}{15}$$

$$\Rightarrow \qquad 20 + x = 64 \Rightarrow x = 64 - 20 = 44 \text{ m}$$

16. (C)

Here $h = 4$ cm

$$2\pi r = 11 \Rightarrow r = \frac{11}{2\pi} = \frac{11 \times 7}{2 \times 22} = \frac{7}{4} \text{ cm}$$

Volume of the cylinder $= \pi r^2 h$

$$= \frac{22}{7} \times \frac{7}{4} \times \frac{7}{4} \times 4$$

$$= \frac{11 \times 7}{2} = \frac{77}{2} = 38.5 \text{ cm}^3$$

17. (C)

Total surface area of cube = 486 (Given)

$$\therefore \qquad 6a^2 = 486$$

where a is side.

$$\Rightarrow \qquad a^2 = 81 \Rightarrow a = 9 \text{ cm}$$

18. (A)

Here $MC = AD = 15$ cm

$AM = DC = 11$ cm

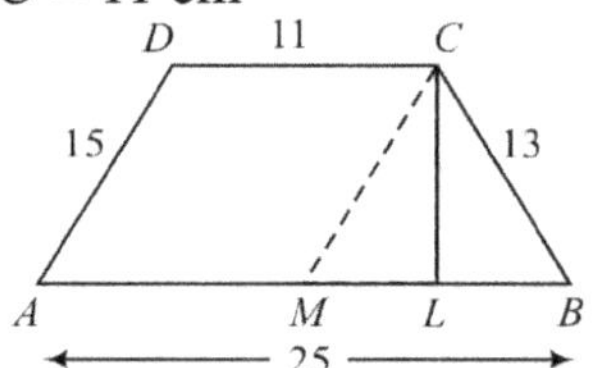

In $\triangle BMC$, $MB = 25 - 11 = 14$

$$S = \frac{13 + 14 + 15}{2} = \frac{42}{2} = 21$$

Area of $\Delta BMC = \sqrt{s\,(s-a)\,(s-b)\,(s-c)}$

$= \sqrt{21 \times 8 \times 7 \times 6}$

$= \sqrt{7 \times 3 \times 4 \times 2 \times 7 \times 3 \times 2}$

$= 7 \times 2 \times 3 \times 2 = 84 \text{ cm}^2$

Now $\quad \dfrac{1}{2} \times CL \times MB = 84$

$\Rightarrow \quad CL = \dfrac{84 \times 2}{14} = 12 \text{ cm}$

$\therefore$ Area of trapezium

$= \dfrac{1}{2}\,(11+25) \times 12 = 36 \times 6 = 216 \text{ cm}^2$

19. (B)

Area of trapezium $= 384$

$\Rightarrow \quad \dfrac{1}{2}\,(5x + 3x)\,12 = 384.$

$\Rightarrow \quad 8x = \dfrac{384 \times 2}{12}$

$\Rightarrow \quad x = \dfrac{32 \times 2}{8} = 8 \text{ cm}$

Parallel sides are 40 cm and 24 cm.

20. (A)

Total area = area of ΔSTR
+ area of square $PQRT$

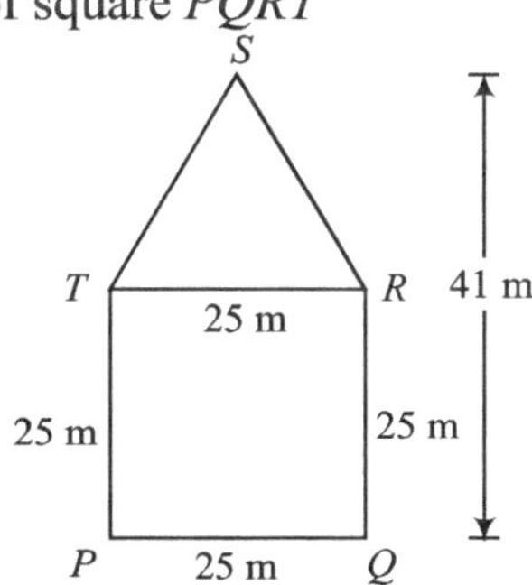

$= \dfrac{1}{2} \times 25 \times (41 - 25) + 25 \times 25$

$= \dfrac{1}{2} \times 25 \times 16 + 625$

$= 200 + 625$

$= 825 \text{ m}^2$

21. (B)

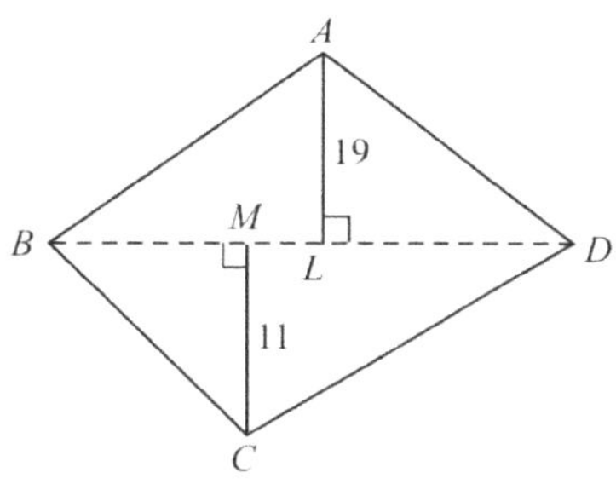

Area of the field

= Area of ΔABD + Area of ΔBCD

$= \dfrac{1}{2} \times 36 \times 19 + \dfrac{1}{2} \times 36 \times 11$

$= 18 \times 19 + 18 \times 11$

$= 18\,(19 + 11)$

$= 18 \times 30 = 540 \text{ m}^2$

22. (A)

Let the length of cube $= a$.
Surface area $= 6a^2$.
New Length of cube $= 2a$.
New Surface area $= 6(2a)^2 = 6 \times 4a^2 = 4 \times 6a^2$

23. (A)

Total surface area of cuboid
$= 2\,(lb + bh + lh)$
$\Rightarrow 2(x \times 2x + 2x \times 3x + x \times 3x) = 88$

$\Rightarrow 2x^2 + 6x^2 + 3x^2 = 44$

$\Rightarrow 11x^2 = 44 \Rightarrow x^2 = 4 \Rightarrow x = 2$

Here $l = 2$ cm
$\quad\quad b = 2 \times 2 = 4$ cm
$\quad\quad h = 3 \times 2 = 6$ cm
$\therefore$ Volume of cuboid $= 2 \times 4 \times 6 = 48 \text{ cm}^3$

24. (B)

Curved surface area of cylinder $= 220$
$\Rightarrow \quad 2\pi rh = 220 \quad \dots(1)$
and volume of cylinder $= 770$
$\quad \pi r^2 h = 770 \quad \dots(2)$

$\therefore \quad \dfrac{\pi r^2 h}{2\pi rh} = \dfrac{770}{220}$

$\Rightarrow \qquad \dfrac{r}{2} = \dfrac{77}{22}$

$\Rightarrow \qquad r = \dfrac{77 \times 2}{22} = 7$ cm

$\therefore$ Diameter $= 2r = 2 \times 7 = 14$ cm.

25. (C)

$2\pi r = 44 \Rightarrow \quad 2 \times \dfrac{22}{7} \times r = 44$

$\Rightarrow \qquad r = \dfrac{7 \times 44}{44} = 7$ cm

and $\quad h = 15$ cm

$\therefore$ Volume of cylinder $= \pi r^2 h$

$\qquad = \dfrac{22}{7} \times 7 \times 7 \times 15$

$\qquad = 22 \times 105$

$\qquad = 2310$ cm^3

HOTS (ACHIEVERS SECTION)

26. (A)	27. (D)	28. (A)	29. (A)	30. (D)

26. (A)
Area of base $= 180$ cm^2

$\pi r^2 = 180$

Volume of cone $= \dfrac{1}{3} \pi r^2 h$

$\qquad = \dfrac{1}{3} \times 180 \times 8 = 480$ cm^3

27. (D)
Curved surface area $= 5940$

$\Rightarrow \qquad 2\pi rh = 5940$

$\Rightarrow \quad 2 \times \dfrac{22}{7} \times r \times 30 = 5940$

$\Rightarrow \quad 2r = \dfrac{5940 \times 7}{22 \times 30} = 63$ cm

28. (A)

$\dfrac{x^0 - y^0}{x^0 + y^0} = \dfrac{1-1}{1+1} = \dfrac{0}{2} = 0$

29. (C)
Let the length be x.

Width $= \dfrac{x}{4} + 2 = \dfrac{x+8}{4}$

Perimeter of rectangle $= 54$

$\Rightarrow \qquad 2\left(x + \dfrac{x+8}{4} \right) = 54$

$\Rightarrow \qquad 2\left(\dfrac{4x + x + 8}{4} \right) = 54$

$\Rightarrow 5x + 8 = 108 \Rightarrow 5x = 100$

$\Rightarrow \qquad x = 20$ cm.

30. (D)
Volume of earth dug out

$\qquad = \pi \left(\dfrac{8}{2} \right)^2 \times 7$

$\qquad = \dfrac{22}{7} \times \left(\dfrac{8}{2} \right)^2 \times 7$

$\qquad = \pi \times 16 \times 7$

$\qquad = 22 \times 16 = 352$ m^3

Area of embankment $= \pi (R^2 - r^2)$

$\qquad = \pi (6^2 - 4^2)$

$\qquad = \pi (36 - 16) = 20\,\pi$ m^3

Area of embankment $\times$ h $=$ volume of earth dug out.

$\Rightarrow \quad 20\pi \times h = 16 \times 7 \times \pi$

$\Rightarrow \quad h = \dfrac{16 \times 7}{20} = 5.6$ m

12. EXPONENTS AND POWERS

Answer Key

1. (B)	2. (C)	3. (B)	4. (C)	5. (B)	6. (D)	7. (D)	8. (D)	9. (A)	10 (A)
11. (C)	12. (B)	13. (C)	14. (A)	15. (D)	16. (B)	17. (C)	18. (D)	19. (C)	20. (B)
21. (C)	22. (A)	23. (C)	24. (D)	25. (D)					

1. **(B)**

We have $(4^{-1} + 8^{-1}) \div \left(\dfrac{2}{3}\right)^{-1}$

$= \left(\dfrac{1}{4} + \dfrac{1}{8}\right) \div \dfrac{1}{\frac{2}{3}} = \dfrac{3}{8} \div \dfrac{3}{2} = \dfrac{3}{8} \times \dfrac{2}{3} = \dfrac{1}{4}$

2. **(C)**

3. **(B)**

Let the number be x.

$$\left(\dfrac{1}{2}\right)^{-1} \times x = \left(\dfrac{-5}{4}\right)^{-1}$$

$\Rightarrow \quad \dfrac{1}{\frac{1}{2}} \times x = \dfrac{1}{\frac{-5}{4}} \Rightarrow 2x = \dfrac{4}{-5}$

$\Rightarrow \quad x = \dfrac{4}{-5 \times 2} = -\dfrac{2}{5}$

4. **(C)**

$(-6)^{-1} \times x = 9^{-1}$

$\Rightarrow \quad \dfrac{1}{-6} \times x = \dfrac{1}{9} \Rightarrow x = \dfrac{-6}{9} = \dfrac{-2}{3}$

5. **(B)**

We have

$0.00000000837 = \dfrac{837}{10^{11}} = \dfrac{837}{100 \times 10^{9}}$

$\qquad = 8.37 \times 10^{-9}$

6. **(D)**

Given

$\left(\dfrac{7}{12}\right)^{-4} \times \left(\dfrac{7}{12}\right)^{3x} = \left(\dfrac{7}{12}\right)^{5}$

$\Rightarrow \quad \left(\dfrac{7}{12}\right)^{3x - 4} = \left(\dfrac{7}{12}\right)^{5}$

$\Rightarrow \quad 3x - 4 = 5 \Rightarrow 3x = 9 \Rightarrow x = 3$

7. **(D)**

Here $(3^{-1} + 4^{-1})^{-1} \div 5^{-1}$

$= \left(\dfrac{1}{3} + \dfrac{1}{4}\right)^{-1} \div 5^{-1}$

$= \left(\dfrac{7}{12}\right)^{-1} \div \dfrac{1}{5}$

$= \dfrac{1}{\frac{7}{12}} \div \dfrac{1}{5}$

$= \dfrac{12}{7} \times \dfrac{5}{1} = \dfrac{60}{7}$

8. **(D)**

Here $(2^{3}x^{-1} + 10) \div 7 = 6$

$\Rightarrow \quad (2^{3x - 1} + 10) \times \dfrac{1}{7} = 6$

$\Rightarrow \quad 2^{3x - 1} + 10 = 42$

$\Rightarrow \quad 2^{3x - 1} = 32 = 2^{5}$

On comparing the powers

$\qquad 3x - 1 = 5 \Rightarrow 3x = 6$

$\Rightarrow \qquad x = 2$

9. **(A)**

$0.000467 \times 10^{4}.$

$= \dfrac{467}{10^{6}} \times 10^{4} = \dfrac{467}{10^{2}} = \dfrac{467}{100} = 4.67$

10. **(A)**

$$\left(\frac{5}{4}\right)^{-2} \div \left(\frac{-5}{4}\right)^{-3} = -\left(\frac{5}{4}\right)^{-2-(-3)}$$

$$= \left(\frac{-5}{4}\right)^{1} = -\left(\frac{4}{5}\right)^{-1}$$

$$= \left(\frac{-4}{5}\right)^{x} \Rightarrow x = -1$$

11. (C)

$$\left[(2)^{\frac{1}{2}}\right]^{4 \times -0.5} = \left[(2)^{\frac{1}{2}}\right]^{-2}$$

$$= [2]^{\frac{1}{2} \times (-2)} = (2)^{-1} = \frac{1}{2}$$

12. (B)

$$1 \text{ micron} = \frac{1}{1000000} \text{ m}$$

$$= 1 \times 10^{-6} \text{m.}$$

13. (C)

$$5^{-3} + 5^{-2} + 5^{-1} + 5^{0}$$

$$= 5^{-1}(5^{-2} + 5^{-1} + 5^{0}) + 5^{0} \quad [\because 5^{0} = 1]$$

$$= 5^{-1}\left(\frac{1}{25} + \frac{1}{5} + 1\right) + 1$$

$$= 5^{-1}\left(\frac{1 + 5 + 25}{25}\right) + 1$$

$$= \frac{31}{125} + 1 = \frac{156}{125} = 1.248$$

14. (A)

Let $5^{p} = t,$

$$\therefore \qquad 5^{2p} + 5^{p} = 650$$

$$\Rightarrow \qquad t^{2} + t - 650 = 0 \Rightarrow t = 25$$

$$\Rightarrow \qquad 5^{p} = 25 \Rightarrow 5^{p} = (5)^{2}$$

$$\Rightarrow \qquad p = 2$$

15. (D)

Given $\dfrac{5^{3}}{5^{2}} = (5)^{3-2} = (5)^{1} = 5$

$$5 \times \frac{2^{5}}{3^{5}} \times \frac{2^{x}}{3^{x}} = 0.0578$$

$$\Rightarrow \quad \frac{2^{x}}{3^{x}} = \left(\frac{2}{3}\right)^{6}$$

$$\Rightarrow \quad x = 6$$

16. (B)

$$(2)^{5} = 32$$

$$\therefore (32)^{2x+1} = ((2)^{5})^{2x+1} = (2)^{10x+5}$$

$$\therefore (2)^{10x+5} = (2)^{-3x}(2)^{-8}$$

$$\Rightarrow \quad 10x + 5 = -3x - 8$$

$$\Rightarrow \quad 13x = -13 \Rightarrow x = -1.$$

17. (C)

$$(23)^{-3} \times x = (69)^{-1}$$

$$x = \frac{23 \times 23 \times 23}{69} = \frac{529}{3}$$

18. (D)

$$\left(5^{-1} + 6^{-1}\right) = \frac{1}{5} + \frac{1}{6} = \frac{11}{30}$$

$$\therefore \qquad k^{-1} = \frac{11}{30} \times \frac{1}{22} = \frac{1}{60}$$

$$\Rightarrow \qquad \frac{1}{k} = \frac{1}{60}$$

$$\Rightarrow \qquad k = 60$$

19. (C)

$$\text{Distance} = 15 \times 10^{7} \text{ km}$$

$$= 15 \times 10^{7} \times 10^{3} \text{ m}$$

$$= 15 \times 10^{10} \text{ m}$$

$$= 1.5 \times 10^{11} \text{ m}$$

20. (B)

$$\left(\frac{25}{16}\right)^{4} = \left(\left(\frac{5}{4}\right)^{2}\right)^{4} = \left(\frac{5}{4}\right)^{2 \times 4} = \left(\frac{5}{4}\right)^{8}.$$

$$\left(\frac{225}{144}\right)^{-3} = \left(\frac{25}{16}\right)^{-3} = \left(\frac{5}{4}\right)^{-2 \times 3} = \left(\frac{5}{4}\right)^{-6}$$

$$\therefore \left(\frac{25}{16}\right)^{4} \div \left(\frac{225}{144}\right)^{-3} = \left(\frac{5}{4}\right)^{14}$$

21. (C)

Here $(6 + 3) \times 9^{-1} \div 3^{-1} + 2^{-2}$

$$= 9 \times 9^{-1} \div 3^{-1} + 2^{-2}$$

22. (A)

$$= 9 \times \frac{1}{3} + 2^{-2} = 3 + \frac{1}{4} = \frac{13}{4}$$

We have $\dfrac{p^m}{p^n} \times \dfrac{n^p}{m^p} \times \dfrac{p^{n+m}}{m^{p+n}}$

$$= p^{m-n+n+m} \times n^p \times m^{-p-p-n}$$

$$= p^{2m} \times n^p \times m^{-2p-n}$$

$\because m = n = p$

$\therefore p^{3p-2p-p} = p^0 = 1$

23. (C)

Size of plant cell $= 1275 \times 10^{-8}$ m

$\qquad = 1.275 \times 10^{-5}$ m.

24. (D)

$$\left(\frac{1}{3}\right)^{-2} = 9, \left(\frac{1}{4}\right)^{-2} = 16$$

$\therefore [9 - 16]^{-2} \times 7^2 = (7)^{-2} \times (7)^2$

$$= (7)^{-2+2}$$

$$= (7)^0 = 1$$

25. (D)

Here $2^{3x+5} \times (3)^{2x+5}$

$$= (2)^{3x+2} \times (3)^{3x+2}$$

$\Rightarrow (2)^{(3x+5-3x-2)} = (3)^{3x+2-2x-5}$

$\Rightarrow \qquad\qquad (2)^3 = (3)^{x-3}$

$\Rightarrow 2^3 = \dfrac{3^x}{3^3}$

$\Rightarrow 3^x = 2^3 \times 3^3$

$\Rightarrow 3^x = 6^3$

$\Rightarrow 3^x = 216$

HOTS (ACHIEVERS SECTION)

26. (A)	27. (A)	28. (C)	29. (A)	30. (A)

26. (A)

$$\frac{2.6 \times 10^8 \times 45}{10} = 117 \times 10^7 = 1.17 \times 10^9$$

27. (A)

$lbh = 3000$

$\Rightarrow \quad 20 \times 12 \times h = 3000$

$\Rightarrow \quad h = \dfrac{3000}{20 \times 12} = 12.5$ cm

13. DIRECT AND INVERSE VARIATIONS

1. (A)	2. (B)	3. (B)	4. (C)	5. (A)	6. (D)	7. (C)	8. (C)	9. (C)	10 (B)
11. (C)	12. (D)	13. (D)	14. (A)	15. (C)	16. (C)	17. (B)	18. (B)	19. (D)	20. (C)
21. (B)	22. (C)	23. (B)	24. (D)	25. (C)					

1. (A)

Speed of train $= 36$ km/hour

$$= 36 \times \frac{5}{18} = 10 \text{ m/sec}$$

$\therefore$ Length of train $= 10 \times 25 = 250$ m.

2. (B)

If x is required no. of days then

Number of men	Number of days
1500	38
1900	x

$\Rightarrow \dfrac{1500}{1900} = \dfrac{x}{38}$

$$x = \frac{1500 \times 38}{1900} = 30 \text{ days}$$

3. **(B)**

If x is bundles can be pack in 7 days then

No. of bundles	No. of days
260	5
x	7

$$\frac{260}{x} = \frac{5}{7} \Rightarrow x = \frac{260 \times 7}{5} = 364$$

4. **(C)**

Let x be required no. of days then

Wages	No. of days
280	8
945	x

$$\frac{8}{x} = \frac{280}{945} \Rightarrow x = \frac{8 \times 945}{280}$$

$$\Rightarrow \qquad x = 27 \text{ days}$$

5. **(A)**

If x is required distance then

Distance	Time (min)
56	60
x	15

$$\frac{56}{x} = \frac{60}{15} \Rightarrow x = \frac{15 \times 56}{60} = 14 \text{ km}$$

6. **(D)**

If x is required no. of days then

No. of days	Mass of dust
15	1.2×10^8
x	4.8×10^8

$$\frac{15}{x} = \frac{1.2 \times 10^8}{4.8 \times 10^8}$$

$$\Rightarrow \quad x = \frac{4.8 \times 10^8 \times 15}{1.2 \times 10^8}$$

$$\Rightarrow \ x = 60 \text{ days.}$$

7. **(C)**

Given

L	M
10	6

Since L and M are inversely proportional

$a_1 b_1 = a_2 b_2 = \ ....$

$10 \times 6 = 60$

$12 \times 5 = 60$

$15 \times 4 = 60$

$45 \times 1.3 = 58.5$

$25 \times 2.4 = 60$

8. **(C)**

If x is required persons then

No. of persons	No. of days
28	65
x	35

It is the case of inverse variation.

$$\therefore \quad \frac{28}{x} = \frac{35}{65} \Rightarrow x = \frac{28 \times 65}{35} = 52$$

9. **(C)**

Here Speed of train $= 81$ km/hour

$$= 81 \times \frac{5}{18} = \frac{45}{2} \text{ m/s}$$

Distance covered $= 270 + 225 = 495$m.

$$\text{Time taken by train} = \frac{495}{\dfrac{45}{2}} = \frac{495 \times 2}{45} = 22 \text{ sec}$$

10. **(B)**

If x is required time then

No. of days	No. of hours
18	8
12	x

$$\therefore \quad \frac{18}{12} = \frac{x}{8} \Rightarrow x = \frac{18 \times 8}{12} = 12 \text{ hours}$$

11. **(C)**

If x is required days then

No. of Men	No. of days
6	8
8	x

$$\frac{6}{8} = \frac{x}{8} \Rightarrow x = \frac{8 \times 6}{8} = 6 \text{ days}$$

12. **(D)**

If x required machines then

OLYMPIAD WORKBOOK (IMO) CLASS – 8

No. of machines	No. of days
42	56
x	48

$$\frac{42}{x} = \frac{48}{56} \Rightarrow x = \frac{42 \times 56}{48} = 49 \text{ machines}$$

13. (D)

Here actual length of bacteria $= \dfrac{7}{70000}$

$$= \frac{1}{10000} = 10^{-4}\,\text{cm}$$

14. (A)

Given 5 men = 7 women

$\therefore$ 1 men $= \dfrac{7}{5}$ women

Now   10 men $= \dfrac{7}{5} \times 10 = 14$ women

If x is required money then

No. of women	Earning (₹)
7	1372
19	x

$$\frac{7}{19} = \frac{1372}{x} \Rightarrow x = \frac{1372 \times 19}{7}$$

$$\Rightarrow \quad x = ₹\,3724$$

15. (C)

If x is required men then

Length	No. of persons
$\dfrac{27}{4}$ m	11
27 m	x

$$\frac{\dfrac{27}{4}}{27} = \frac{11}{x}$$

$$\Rightarrow \quad x = \frac{27 \times 11 \times 4}{27} = 44 \text{ men}$$

16. (C)

If x is actual distance then

Distance on map (cm)	1	5

Actual distance (cm)	3×10^7	x

$$x = \frac{5 \times 3 \times 10^7}{100 \times 1000}\,\text{km} = 1500 \text{ km}$$

17. (B)

If x is required distance then

Time (Sec)	Distance
$\dfrac{35}{60}$	18
7	x

$$\frac{\dfrac{35}{60}}{7} = \frac{18}{x} \Rightarrow x = \frac{18 \times 7 \times 60}{35}$$

$$\Rightarrow \quad x = 216 \text{ km}$$

18. (B)

If x is required no. of days then

No. of cows	No. of days
6	28
21	x

It is the case of inverse variation.

$$\Rightarrow \quad \frac{6}{21} = \frac{x}{28} \Rightarrow x = \frac{28 \times 6}{21} = 8 \text{ days}$$

19. (D)

If x is required distance then

Time (min)	Distance (km)
60	84
15	x

$$\therefore \quad \frac{60}{15} = \frac{84}{x} \Rightarrow x = \frac{84 \times 15}{60} = 21 \text{ km}$$

20. (C)

If x is required number of words then

Time (min)	No. of words
30	510
10	x

$$\Rightarrow \quad \frac{30}{10} = \frac{510}{x}$$

$$x = \frac{510 \times 10}{30} = 170 \text{ words}$$

21. (B)

If x is required number of days then

No. of workers	No. of days
14	42
21	x

It is case of inverse variation.

$$\therefore \quad \frac{14}{21} = \frac{x}{42} \Rightarrow x = \frac{14 \times 42}{21} = 28 \text{ days}$$

22. (C)

In 1 day (A + B) can do $\left(\dfrac{1}{25} + \dfrac{1}{20}\right)$ part of work.

$$= \frac{4+5}{100} = \frac{9}{100} \text{ part of work}$$

In 5 days (A + B) can do $\dfrac{9 \times 5}{100}$ part of work.

$$= \frac{9}{20} \text{ part of work}$$

Remaining part $= 1 - \dfrac{9}{20} = \dfrac{11}{20}$

B can finish the remaining work in $\dfrac{11}{20} \times 20$

$= 11$ days

23. (B)

In one day (Amar + Rajesh + Mohan) can do

$$\frac{1}{10} + \frac{1}{12} + \frac{1}{15} = \frac{6+5+4}{60}$$

$$= \frac{15}{60} = \frac{1}{4}$$

So, they can finish the work in 4 days if they work together.

24. (D)

Here $\dfrac{1}{9} - \dfrac{1}{10} = \dfrac{10-9}{90} = \dfrac{1}{90}$

So, cistern will be emptied by the leak in 90 hours.

HOTS (ACHIEVERS SECTION)

26. (A)	27. (C)	28. (B)	29. (D)	30. (B)

14. FACTORISATION

1. (B)	2. (A)	3. (D)	4. (B)	5. (A)	6. (B)	7. (C)	8. (D)	9. (A)	10 (B)
11. (B)	12. (D)	13. (A)	14. (D)	15. (A)	16. (A)	17. (C)	18. (B)	19. (D)	20. (D)

HOTS (ACHIEVERS SECTION)

21. (C)	22. (D)	23. (A)	24. (C)	25. (B)

15. INTRODUCTION TO GRAPHS

1. (C)	2. (D)	3. (A)	4. (C)	5. (B)	6. (A)	7. (D)	8. (B)	9. (A)	10 (C)
11. (D)	12. (C)	13. (C)	14. (B)	15. (A)	16. (B)	17. (A)	18. (D)	19. (A)	20. (C)

21. (C)	22. (B)	23. (B)	24. (A)	25. (B)

16. PLAYING WITH NUMBERS

1. (C)	2. (B)	3. (A)	4. (B)	5. (C)	6. (B)	7. (B)	8. (B)	9. (A)	10 (B)
11. (A)	12. (C)	13. (B)	14. (D)	15. (A)	16. (D)	17. (B)	18. (A)	19. (C)	20. (D)

1. **(C)**
   $182 \times 22 = 4004$
   $\therefore \quad a = 4$

2. **(B)**
   $7^1 = 7$
   $7^2 = 49$
   $7^3 = 343$
   $7^4 = 2401$
   $7^5 = 16807$

   $\therefore$ After leaving 4 exponents 7^n repeats its unit digit.
   $\therefore 7^{4n}$ has 1 as its units place digit.
   $\therefore 7^{332}$ has 1 as units place digit.
   $\therefore 7^{333}$ has 7 as its units place digit.

3. **(A)**
   If, sum of digits at odd place
   $\qquad$ = Sum of digits at even place.
   Then , the number will be divisible by 11.
   1221 is divisible by 11

4. **(B)**

   $$\begin{array}{r} 4\,5\,1\,8 \\ +\,2\,y\,7\,7 \\ \hline 7\,3\,x\,5 \end{array}$$

   When 8 and 7 are added, 1 is carry.
   $\therefore \quad x = 7 + 1 + 1 = 9$
   The carry of sum $(5 + y)$ should be 1.
   $\therefore \quad 5 + y = 13$
   $\Rightarrow \quad y = 8$

   $\therefore \quad x + y = 17$

5. **(C)**

   $$\begin{array}{r} a\,a \\ \times\,a\,a \\ \hline a^2\,a^2 \\ a^2\,a^2\,\times \\ \hline a^2\,2a^2a^2 \end{array} \qquad \begin{array}{r} a\,x \\ \times\,a\,a \\ \hline b\,8\,b \end{array}$$

   $\Rightarrow a^2 + a^2 = 8$
   $\Rightarrow 2a^2 = 8$
   $\Rightarrow a = 2, b = 4$
   $\therefore \quad a \times b = 8$

6. **(B)**
   For a number to be divisible by 9, the sum of its digits should be divisible by 9.
   $\therefore \quad 7 + 6 + 3 + * + 3 + 1 + 2 = 22 + *.$
   $\therefore$ 5 should be written on place of * to make the number divisible by 9.

7. **(B)**
   76215*
   $\Rightarrow$ Sum of digits at odd places
   $= * + 1 + 6 = * + 7$
   Sum of digits at even places $= 5 + 2 + 7$
   $\qquad\qquad\qquad\qquad\qquad = 14$
   For divisibility with 11,
   $\qquad\qquad * + 7 = 14$
   $\Rightarrow \qquad\qquad * = 7$

8. **(B)**
   $3c = x\,B$, where, x is the carry,
   $\therefore x + 3B = y\,B$, where y is the carry.
   $\therefore y + 3A = B.$

$\therefore C = 8, B = 4, A = 1.$

$$\begin{array}{r} y\ x \\ A\ B\ C \\ A\ B\ C \\ +\ A\ B\ C \\ \hline B\ B\ C \\ \hline \end{array}$$

9. (A)

Sum of first 22 even natural numbers

$= (2 + 4 + \ldots\ldots + 44)$

$= 2(1 + 2 + \ldots\ldots + 22)$

$= 2 \times \dfrac{22 \times 23}{2}$

$= 2 \times 11 \times 23$

$= 22 \times 23 = 506$

10. (B)

Suppose the candles have burnt for 'x' hours,

$$\left(1 - \frac{x}{6}\right) = 2 \times \left(1 - \frac{x}{2}\right)$$

$\Rightarrow \qquad x = \dfrac{6}{5}$ hours.

11. (A)

735 is a number having all its digits as prime number and all the digits of 735 are the factors of 735.

12. (C)

5	x	e	d
16	y	7	c
a	13	b	6
2	z	9	f

We have to find, the value of

$(a + b + c + d + e) + (x + y + z) + f = p$

$\because$ Sum of numbers of any row/column $= 34$

$\therefore \quad a + b + 13 + 6 = x + y + z + 13$

$= e + b + 7 + 9 = c + d + 6 + f$

$= 5 + 16 + a + 2 = x + e + d + 5$

$= 16 + y + 7 + c = 2 + z + 9 + f = 34$

$\Rightarrow 2(a + b + c + d + e + f + x + y + z)$

$+ 19 + 13 + 16 + 6 + 23 + 5$

$\qquad + 23 + 11 = 34 \times 8$

$\Rightarrow \qquad 2p + 116 = 272$

$\Rightarrow \qquad\qquad p = 78$

13. (B)

Let the three natural numbers be x, y and z.

$\therefore \quad \dfrac{x + y + z}{3} \geq (xyz)^{\frac{1}{3}} \qquad\qquad [\text{AM} \geq \text{GM}]$

$\Rightarrow \qquad \dfrac{10}{3} \geq (xyz)^{\frac{1}{3}}$

$\Rightarrow \qquad xyz \leq \dfrac{1000}{27}$

$\Rightarrow \qquad xyz \leq 37.03$

$\therefore$ The limiting value of xyz is 37.03,

$\because$ The numbers x, y and z are natural.

$\therefore$ 37.03 cannot be obtained as a product.

$\because$ 37 is a prime number.

$\therefore$ 36 is the greatest number which can be obtained as a product of 3 natural numbers whose sum is 10.

14. (D)

$6^0 = 1$

$6^1 = 6$

$6^2 = 36$

$6^3 = 216$

$6^4 = 1296$

$6^5 = 7776$

$\therefore$ It is observed that 6^n has 6 at its units place.

$\therefore 6^{222}$ has 6 as its unit's place digit.

15. (A)

$1729 = (12)^3 + (1)^3$

$\therefore$ 1729 can be expressed as sum of two perfect natural cubes.

It is the smallest number to satisfy this condition, and, is known as Ramanujan's Number.

16. (D)

$$\begin{array}{r} y\ x \\ P\ A\ T \\ +\ E\ A\ T \\ \hline F\ E\ E\ A \\ \hline \end{array}$$

x, y are respective carries.

$\qquad y + P + E = F E$

$\qquad x + 2A = y E$

$T + T = x A$

$\Rightarrow P = 9, A = 8, T = 4, E = 6$ and $F = 1$

$\therefore \qquad F = 1$

17. **(B)**

$xyz = x + y + z$ ...(i)

We also know that,

$$\left(\frac{x + y + z}{3}\right)^3 \geq xyz$$

$$\left(\frac{x + y + z}{3}\right)^3 - (x + y + z) \geq 0$$

$$(x + y + z)\left(\frac{(x + y + z)^2}{9} - 1\right) \geq 0$$

$$(x + y + z)\left(\frac{(x + y + z)^2 - 9}{9}\right) \geq 0$$

$$(x + y + z)(x + y + z - 3)(x + y + z + 3) \geq 0$$

$\therefore$ Sum of 3 natural numbers > 3.

$\therefore$ Required set of natural numbers $= (1, 2, 3)$.

18. **(A)**

$\because$ Last (unit) place digit $= 5$

$\therefore$ The least natural number whose perfect square is having 5, as its unit place digit will be equal to 5.

$\therefore \quad 5^2 = 25$

19. **(C)**

135×135

Trick :

$135 \times 135 = 25$

Multiply the units place 5 and write the product, Add 1 to any one of the remaining digits at tenths place and write the product on tenths place.

$13 \times 14 = 182$

$\therefore \ 135 \times 135 = 18225$

20. **(D)**

$\because$ Perfect squares should have 1, 4, 9, 6 and 5 as their units place digit.

$\therefore$ 1282 is not a perfect square.

HOTS (ACHIEVERS SECTION)

21. (A)	22. (B)	23. (B)	24. (B)	25. (A)

21. **(A)**

Probability of getting 2 or 3 heads

$$= \frac{3}{8} + \frac{1}{8} = \frac{1}{2} = 0.5$$

22. **(B)**

$$\frac{65 \times 28}{35} = 52 \ \text{men}$$

23. **(B)**

Let unit's digit $= x$.

$10's$ digit $= (9 - x)$

Number $= 10(9 - x) + 1 \times x$

$= 90 - 10x + x = 90 - 9x$

Given $90 - 9x - 9 = 10x + 1(9 - x)$

$81 - 9x = 10x + 9 - x = 9x + 9$

$9x + 9x = 81 - 9$

$\Rightarrow \ 18x = 72 \Rightarrow x = \dfrac{72}{18} = 4$

Number $= 90 - 9 \times 4$

$= 90 - 36 = 54.$

Half $= \dfrac{54}{2} = 27$

24. **(B)**

Let the numbers be x and y.

$\therefore \ xy = 1575$, and, $\dfrac{x}{y} = \dfrac{9}{7}$

From, $\dfrac{x}{y} = \dfrac{9}{7}, \Rightarrow x = \dfrac{9y}{7}$

$\therefore \quad \dfrac{9y}{7} \times y = 1575$

$\Rightarrow \ y^2 = \dfrac{1575 \times 7}{9} = 175 \times 7 = 25 \times 7 \times 7$

$\Rightarrow \ y = 5 \times 7 = 35, x = 45$

$\therefore$ Difference of numbers $= 45 - 35 = 10$

Answer Key

1. (C)	2. (D)	3. (C)	4. (A)	5. (D)	6. (B)	7. (A)	8. (B)	9. (B)	10. (B)
11. (C)	12. (A)	13. (A)	14. (C)	15. (B)	16. (C)	17. (A)	18. (B)	19. (C)	20. (A)
21. (A)	22. (C)	23. (D)	24. (B)	25. (A)	26. (C)	27. (D)	28. (C)	29. (A)	30. (D)
31. (D)	32. (A)	33. (A)	34. (C)	35. (A)	36. (B)	37. (D)	38. (A)	39. (D)	40. (A)

1. **(C)**

   $Z = 26$; $O = 15$.

   $ZOO = 26 + 15 + 15 = 56$.

   $D = 4$, $E = 5$; $R = 18$.

   $DEER = 4 + 5 + 5 + 18 = 32$.

   $LION = 12 + 9 + 15 + 14 = 50$

2. **(D)**

   $JEANS = 10 + 5 + 1 + 14 + 19 = 49$.

   $COAT = 3 + 15 + 1 + 20 = 39$.

   $SHIRT = 19 + 8 + 9 + 18 + 20 = 74$

3. **(C)**

   $BUD = 2 + 21 + 4 = 27$

   $ROSE = 18 + 15 + 19 + 5 = 57$

   $FLOWER = 6 + 12 + 15 + 23 + 5 + 18 = 79$

4. **(A)**

   Spanner is used by carpenter and all other tools are used by gardener.

5. **(D)**

   All except oasis are related to sea.

6. **(B)**

   All except Appendix are bones of our body.

7. **(A)**

   In this code, a letter is the nth letter from the beginning of English alphabet then in the code the corresponding letter is the nth letter from the end.

   HAND → SZMW

   then MILK → NROP

8. **(B)**

   T U R N
   +2↓ +2↓ +2↓ +2↓
   V W T P

   Similarly W A L K
   +2↓ +2↓ +2↓ +2↓
   Y C N M

9. **(B)**

   G U A V A
   +1↓ +1↓ +1↓ +1↓ +1↓
   H V B W B

   Similarly J U I C E
   +1↓ +1↓ +1↓ +1↓ +1↓
   K V J D F

10. **(B)**

    Starting position of Nitesh is A and his final position is F which is in the South-East direction from starting point.

    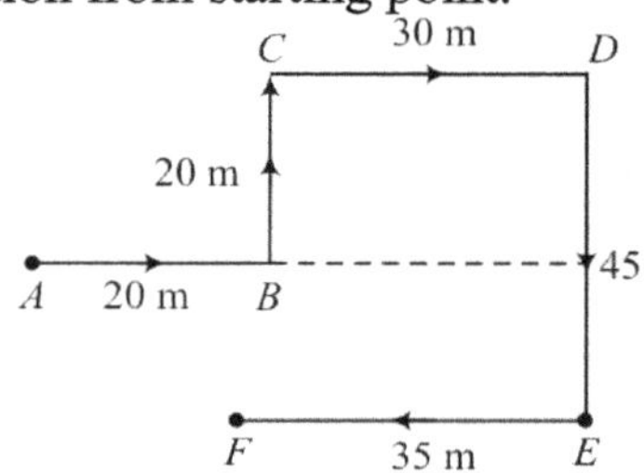

11. **(C)**

    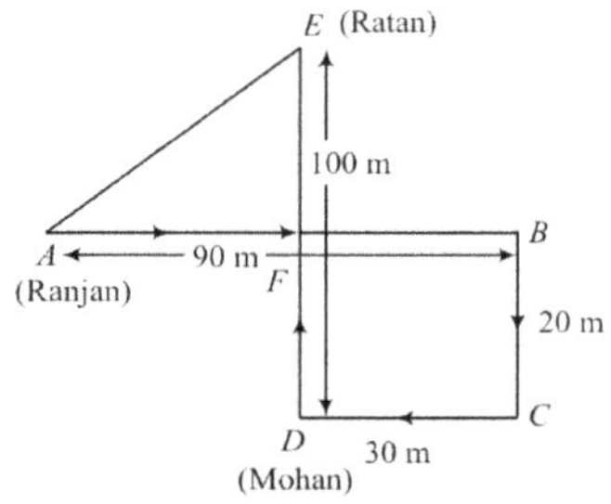

    In the Fig, A is Ranjan's position and E is Ratan's position. The required distance = AE

    $$AE = \sqrt{(AF)^2 + EF^2}$$

    $$= \sqrt{(90 - 30)^2 + (100 - 20)^2}$$

    $$= \sqrt{3600 + 6400} = 100 \text{ m}$$

12. **(A)**

OLYMPIAD WORKBOOK (IMO) CLASS – 8

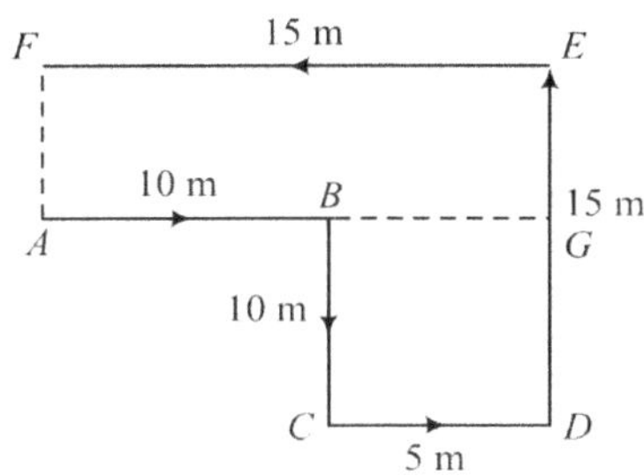

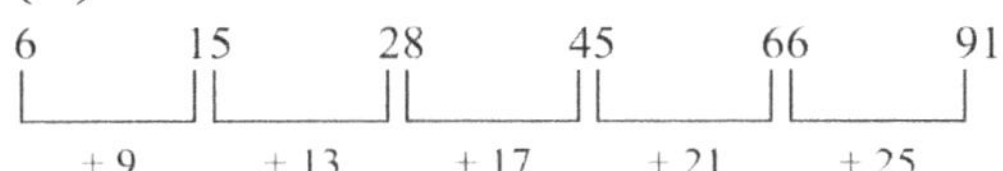

Dinesh starts from A and his final position is at F.

$AF = DE - GD = 15 - 10 = 5$ m

13. (A)

$$6 \quad 15 \quad 28 \quad 45 \quad 66 \quad 91$$
$$+9 \quad +13 \quad +17 \quad +21 \quad +25$$

14. (C)

$$12 \quad 19 \quad 28 \quad 39 \quad 52 \quad 67$$
$$+7 \quad +9 \quad +11 \quad +13 \quad +15$$

15. (B)

$$10 \quad 22 \quad 46 \quad 94 \quad 190$$
$$+12 \quad +24 \quad +48 \quad +96$$

16. (C)

$(5 + 6 + 7) \times 3 = 18 \times 3 = 54$

$(7 + 11 + 8) \times 3 = 26 \times 3 = 78$

$\therefore ? = (8 + 12 + 9) \times 3 = 29 \times 3 = 87$

17. (A)

$$\frac{134 - 102}{4} = \frac{32}{4} = 8$$

$$\frac{227 - 143}{4} = \frac{84}{4} = 21$$

$$\therefore ? = \frac{198 - 154}{4} = \frac{44}{4} = 11$$

18. (B)

$4^2 + 5^2 = 16 + 25 = 41$

$12^2 + 8^2 = 144 + 64 = 208$

$\Rightarrow 24^2 + x^2 = 832 \Rightarrow x^2 = 832 - 576 = 256$

$\Rightarrow \quad x = 16$

19. (C)

5 1 4 7 3 9 8 5 7 2 6 3 1 5 8 6 3 8 5 2 2 4 3 ·
4 9 6

20. (A)

5 1 4 7 3 2 5 6 8 9 6 7 3 2 1 5 6 4 3 2 7 4

21. (A)

8 4 7 6 5 3 2 5 1 6 4 3 2 6 7 9 8 5

22. (C)

$12 + 8 + 4 + 4 = 28$

23. (D)

$8 + 10 + 5 + 2 + 1 + 1 = 27.$

24. (B)

$6 + 6 + 2 + 1 = 15$

37. (D)

There are three types of faces, hands and legs. Each type is used once in each row.

38. (A)

The 2nd figure is obtained from the first figure by reversing the direction of RHS arrow and 3rd figure is obtained from second figure by reversing the direction of e ach arrow.

MODEL TEST PAPER

Answer Key

1. (B)	2. (B)	3. (A)	4. (D)	5. (D)	6. (C)	7. (C)	8. (B)	9. (A)	10. (B)
11. (D)	12. (A)	13. (B)	14. (D)	15. (B)	16. (B)	17. (C)	18. (B)	19. (D)	20. (C)
21. (A)	22. (C)	23. (B)	24. (D)	25. (D)	26. (B)	27. (A)	28. (C)	29. (D)	30. (C)
31. (A)	32. (C)	33. (C)	34. (C)	35. (C)	36. (B)	37. (D)	38. (C)	39. (C)	40. (C)
41. (D)	42. (C)	43. (A)	44. (D)	45. (A)	46. (C)	47. (A)	48. (C)	49. (A)	50. (D)

1. STUDENT NAME (IN ENGLISH CAPITAL LETTERS ONLY)

Students must write and darken the respective circles completely using HB Pencil only. Othewise their Answer Sheets will not be evaluated.

PERSONAL DETAILS

2. SCHOOL CODE

3. CLASS

4. SECTION

5. ROLL NO.

6. QUESTION PAPER SET

A ○
B ○
C ○
D ○

7. MOBILE NUMBER

8. GENDER

MALE ○
FEMALE ○

9. STREAM
(Only for Class XI and XII Students)

MATHEMATICS ○
BIOLOGY ○
OTHERS ○

MARK YOUR ANSWERS

No.	A B C D	No.	A B C D
1.	Ⓐ Ⓑ Ⓒ Ⓓ	26.	Ⓐ Ⓑ Ⓒ Ⓓ
2.	Ⓐ Ⓑ Ⓒ Ⓓ	27.	Ⓐ Ⓑ Ⓒ Ⓓ
3.	Ⓐ Ⓑ Ⓒ Ⓓ	28.	Ⓐ Ⓑ Ⓒ Ⓓ
4.	Ⓐ Ⓑ Ⓒ Ⓓ	29.	Ⓐ Ⓑ Ⓒ Ⓓ
5.	Ⓐ Ⓑ Ⓒ Ⓓ	30.	Ⓐ Ⓑ Ⓒ Ⓓ
6.	Ⓐ Ⓑ Ⓒ Ⓓ	31.	Ⓐ Ⓑ Ⓒ Ⓓ
7.	Ⓐ Ⓑ Ⓒ Ⓓ	32.	Ⓐ Ⓑ Ⓒ Ⓓ
8.	Ⓐ Ⓑ Ⓒ Ⓓ	33.	Ⓐ Ⓑ Ⓒ Ⓓ
9.	Ⓐ Ⓑ Ⓒ Ⓓ	34.	Ⓐ Ⓑ Ⓒ Ⓓ
10.	Ⓐ Ⓑ Ⓒ Ⓓ	35.	Ⓐ Ⓑ Ⓒ Ⓓ
11.	Ⓐ Ⓑ Ⓒ Ⓓ	36.	Ⓐ Ⓑ Ⓒ Ⓓ
12.	Ⓐ Ⓑ Ⓒ Ⓓ	37.	Ⓐ Ⓑ Ⓒ Ⓓ
13.	Ⓐ Ⓑ Ⓒ Ⓓ	38.	Ⓐ Ⓑ Ⓒ Ⓓ
14.	Ⓐ Ⓑ Ⓒ Ⓓ	39.	Ⓐ Ⓑ Ⓒ Ⓓ
15.	Ⓐ Ⓑ Ⓒ Ⓓ	40.	Ⓐ Ⓑ Ⓒ Ⓓ
16.	Ⓐ Ⓑ Ⓒ Ⓓ	41.	Ⓐ Ⓑ Ⓒ Ⓓ
17.	Ⓐ Ⓑ Ⓒ Ⓓ	42.	Ⓐ Ⓑ Ⓒ Ⓓ
18.	Ⓐ Ⓑ Ⓒ Ⓓ	43.	Ⓐ Ⓑ Ⓒ Ⓓ
19.	Ⓐ Ⓑ Ⓒ Ⓓ	44.	Ⓐ Ⓑ Ⓒ Ⓓ
20.	Ⓐ Ⓑ Ⓒ Ⓓ	45.	Ⓐ Ⓑ Ⓒ Ⓓ
21.	Ⓐ Ⓑ Ⓒ Ⓓ	46.	Ⓐ Ⓑ Ⓒ Ⓓ
22.	Ⓐ Ⓑ Ⓒ Ⓓ	47.	Ⓐ Ⓑ Ⓒ Ⓓ
23.	Ⓐ Ⓑ Ⓒ Ⓓ	48.	Ⓐ Ⓑ Ⓒ Ⓓ
24.	Ⓐ Ⓑ Ⓒ Ⓓ	49.	Ⓐ Ⓑ Ⓒ Ⓓ
25.	Ⓐ Ⓑ Ⓒ Ⓓ	50.	Ⓐ Ⓑ Ⓒ Ⓓ

Signature of the Student & Date of Examination

Signature of the Invigilator & Date of Examination

V&S Publishers, F-2/16 Ansari Road, Daryaganj, New Delhi-110002, ☎ 011-23240026-27
✉ info@vspublishers.com, 🌐 www.vspublishers.com